# THE *Call* OF

# *Timothy*

Prayers Crafted By,
Crystal City House of Prayer

Year of Intercession...

Jesus teach us to pray...

# TABLE OF CONTENTS

TABLE OF CONTENTS

## SPECIAL THANKS

Crystal City House of Prayer would like to acknowledge and thank Jesus, our great intercessor, who is forever interceding on our behalf, the Holy Spirit who teaches us how to pray and prays through us when we do not know what to say, and to the greatest Father who will ever exist! Thank You Abba for hearing us when we pray. To You, the Great I AM, we say thank you for loving us so well and for tearing the veil, so that we may openly come to you without ceasing. To You be all the honour and glory and praise!

# DEDICATION

This book is dedicated to the youth in the
Municipality of Louise, Manitoba, Canada.  God
has a great plan for your lives!  You really are
the generation that the prophets from long ago
have longed to see arise!

## OUR PRAYER FOR YOU

May we journey together in prayer and intercession for the youth in this generation as one, just as our heavenly Father is One. Abba, make us one as You are One, that we may see Your glory and be with You where You are. Holy Spirit, we ask that You breathe on us, so that we may pray without ceasing and love without limits as we lift an entire generation of youth to You. LORD may this be the Timothy Generation that will not let anyone look down on them because they are young, but rather they would set an example for the believers in speech, in conduct, in love, in faith and in purity. In the Mighty and Glorious Name of JESUS, Amen.

But we will give ourselves continually to

# PRAYER

and to the ministry of the word.   Acts 6:4

# WHO IS TIMOTHY?

The words that Paul wrote in his letters to Timothy are very powerful and personal, but they also paint a glowing picture of someone who became quite important to Paul both ministerially as well as personally. Growing up in Lystra, Timothy's mother and grandmother were faithful Jewish women who had heard Paul preach about Jesus, and had accepted him; as did Timothy. When Paul returned to Lystra a few years later on his second journey, He received a favorable report of Timothy's faith from the brothers at Lystra and Iconium (Acts 16:2) and Paul immediately enlists Timothy to travel with him. From there, the rest of Timothy's story is thoroughly biblically documented as he helps Paul establish churches at Philippi, Thessalonica and Berea (Acts 16:1-17:14). Timothy quickly became an integral part of Paul's missionary journeys and when it came time for Paul to set sail for Athens, he left Timothy behind in Berea, only to later send word for Timothy and Silas to join him (Acts 17:13-15). Timothy was even sent to Thessalonica to strengthen the faith of the church Paul established there (1 Thessalonians 3:1-2). Timothy served alongside Paul for 3 years while they taught the church in Ephesus about the amazing power of God and the significance of Jesus Christ. When Paul was imprisoned for two years in Rome, Timothy served faithfully by his side (Acts 28:16-30). After Paul's release from prison in Rome, Timothy and Paul traveled to Ephesus, only to discover that some men in the Ephesian church were speaking evil of The Way before the multitude (Acts 19:9). Paul desperately needed to reach Macedonia, but he did not want to leave the church in Ephesus in turmoil. Paul's solution to this problem was to leave Timothy behind and to charge him to teach the truth to the church in Ephesus, while he traveled on to Macedonia (1 Timothy 1:3-4). Paul expected to not be delayed in Macedonia and to return shortly to Ephesus. When this did not happen, he wrote Timothy a letter to ensure that "order & truth" be restored to the Ephesian church. Paul's first letter to Timothy outlined the authority to order worship (1 Timothy 2: 1-15), how to appoint elders and deacons (1 Timothy 3:1-3), as well as a warning about false teachers (1 Timothy 6:2-10). Paul's second letter to Timothy was more personal, reminding him to guard his spiritual heritage (2 Timothy 1:4-6), and to keep preaching the Word of God that corrects, rebukes and exhorts all believers (2 Timothy 4:1-5). It is made very clear throughout scripture that Paul thought of Timothy not only as a very faithful friend, but also as his spiritual son; a title he used to describe Timothy on six occasions in his letters (1 Timothy 1:2, 1 Timothy 1:18, 2 Timothy 1:2, 2 Timothy 2:1, 1 Corinthians 4:17). Timothy, only a teenager when recruited by Paul, is a wonderful example of what the youth can do when they let God fully capture their heart. I hope you are richly blessed by the example laid down by those who will undertake the call of Timothy!

# KEY SCRIPTURES FROM TIMOTHY

1 Timothy 4:12-14
Don't let anyone look down on you because you are young, but set an example for the believers in speech, in conduct, in love, in faith and in purity. Until I come, devote yourself to the public reading of Scripture, to preaching and to teaching. Do not neglect your gift, which was given you through prophecy when the body of elders laid their hands on you.

1Timothy 6:11-12
But as for you, O man of God, flee these things. Pursue righteousness, godliness, faith, love, steadfastness, gentleness.  Fight the good fight of the faith. Take hold of the eternal life to which you were called and about which you made the good confession in the presence of many witnesses.

2 Timothy 2:15
Be diligent to present yourself approved to God as a workman who does not need to be ashamed, accurately handling the word of truth.

2 Timothy 3:12
Indeed, all who desire to live a godly life in Christ Jesus will be persecuted.

2 Timothy 3:16-17
All Scripture is God-breathed and is useful for teaching, rebuking, correcting and training in righteousness, so that the servant of God may be thoroughly equipped for every good work.

# ANTITHESIS
## 2 Timothy 3:2-5

**The End Time Church Will Be...**

Lovers Of God

Money Will Have No Hold On Them

Humble

Meek

Modest

Kind

Obedient To Parents

Grateful

Holy

Loving

Forgiving

Building Up Others

Self-controlled

Gentle

They Will Love Good

They Are Loyal

Watchful & On Guard

Caring About Others More Than Themselves

Patient Lovers Of God!

Will Walk In Godliness & The Power Of God

**Run To Ones Such As These!**

THE ANTITHESIS

# OUR PERSONAL NOTE TO YOU

We wanted to share with you this prayer journey
that we began after meeting a group of amazing
youth at the Ministry House. We felt the LORD
asked us to journal what we were praying for
them as well as the youth in this generation.
God has created a great story for each of their
lives and we have been honoured to be called to
pray for them. We hope that it will be an
encouragement to you and a tool that you can
use to pray for the youth in your local area,
country and in the world! There are also
"Notes" pages at the back of this book for you to
craft your own prayers or document anything
God has shared with you as you journey through
prayer for this generation. We also encourage
you to use the extra space on the prayer pages
for journaling. Our hope is that the youth will be
touched by God and encounter the King of kings
causing a radical shift in this generation towards
holiness, righteousness and maturity like we
have never seen before. We pray this journal
will bring you intensity in love, hope and
encouragement as you grow in faith and intimacy
with God for His glory and great JOY.

s the Saviour
cially of those who
mand and teach these things
on't let anyone look down on
u because you are young, but set
n example for the believers in
speech, in conduct, in love, in faith
and in purity. 13 Until I come, devote
yourself to the public reading of
Scripture, to preaching and to
teaching. 14 Do not neglect your gift,
which was given you through
ophecy when the body of elders

*Let* THE *Journey*

*Begin . . .*

Name Meaning:
tim·o·thy
ˈtiməTHē
*honouring God*
Τιμοθεος
(Timotheos)

Timothy
Generation
ARISE!

Praying For:
• The Youth in this
  generation
• Holiness, strength,
  righteousness,
  courage, honour
• God to be glorified
• Love to increase

PASSION
TRUTH
LOVE

Key Scriptures:
• 1 & 2 Timothy

JOEL 2:28

KING

# GENERATION ARISE

Father we pray that You would continue to use us to lay hands on the youth to impart spiritual gifts and to strengthen and establish them. Abba, please keep them hidden from the snares of the enemy and his schemes. Raise up warriors, O God, for Your glory. Holy Spirit may we be the ones who will not fail You as generations past, rather make us one as You are One, so that we will be with You where You are and see Your glory. Do it God! Do it for Your name's sake and for Your Righteousness! Jesus, we pray that You would keep these youth hidden from the enemy's schemes. Just as You kept Peter from the Jewish people, and he declared "Now I know without a doubt that the Lord has sent his angel and rescued me from Herod's clutches," the youth will declare, "Without a doubt the Lord has been with me!" Glory be to God!

(Romans 1:11, John 17:24, Acts 12:11,
Ephesians 3:20-21)

## KNOWLEDGE

Jesus may the youth decree, "It is no longer
because of what you said that we believe, for we
have heard for ourselves, and we know that this
is indeed the Savior of the world." Jesus, let the
youth see and know the truth for themselves,
that You are the Way, the Truth and the Life
and that no one comes to the Father except
through You alone, Jesus. Let them know the
Truth that sets them free.

(John 4:42, John 8:32)

# REST

Thank You Father that the trees of the field shall yield their fruit, and the earth shall yield its increase, and the youth shall be secure in their land. Thank You that they shall know that You are the LORD, when You break the bars of their yoke and deliver them from the hand of those who enslaved them. They shall no more be a prey to the nations, nor shall the beasts of the land devour them. They shall dwell securely, and none shall make them afraid. Thank You that You will provide for them renowned plantations, so that they shall no more be consumed with hunger in the land and no longer suffer the reproach of the nations. They shall know that You are the LORD their God who is with them and that they are Your people, for You, Lord GOD, have declared it. Thank You that You have called them Your sheep- human sheep of Your pasture- and You are their God.

(Ezekiel 34:27-31)

# PURSUIT

Father set Your rule and reign in the youth in this region. God give them dreams and visions of the awakening. Set Your fire in their hearts to pursue You relentlessly. God compel them by Your great love! O Lord may Your loving-kindness and compassion draw each one deep into Your heart that they would have an overwhelming desire to pursue You, Your kingdom and Your righteousness. May they be the generation to birth forth Your will and Your dream for this region. Please protect them as they are being drawn and let not the enemy use those of influence in their lives to quench what You are doing, but rather put logs on the fire. Since they are receiving an unshakable kingdom, let each one be filled with gratitude, and worship You acceptably with reverence and awe; for our God is a consuming fire.

(Matthew 6:33, Hebrews 12:28-29)

DAY 4

# DRAWING

God as Your fellow workers, we pray that the
youth will not receive Your grace in vain, for
You say that in the time of favor You heard
them and in the day of salvation You helped
them. We decree that now is the time of favor,
now is the day of salvation! Abba, You are a
faithful Daddy. You are Love, and we thank
You that You will never leave nor forsake any of
the youth. Papa, You are drawing each one, and
we pray that You would draw each one into
Your arms and give them a desire to sit at the
Father's feet and hear the treasures that You
have for them. In a society that is so busy, may
You raise up a new kind of culture, a Kingdom
Culture, to be at rest and sit at Your feet. Thank
you for preparing the way in the hearts of the
youth and that what You started You will bring
to completion! Thank You that You have
created the youth to be partners in grace when
You called them, and Papa give them the
strength they will need to walk in it. Thank You
for being faithful and speaking Your truth! You
are Amazing!!!

(2 Corinthians 6:1-2, Luke 10:38-42,
Philippians 1:6-7)

DAY 6

## CONSECRATION

God, thank You for choosing the youth for such
a time as this!  Lord, we pray that You will draw
them to a consecrated fast, that they would
proclaim a solemn assembly, that they would
come to the House of the LORD our God and
cry out to the LORD for the day of the LORD is
near!  Freedom comes from You God, because
where the Spirit of the Lord is, there is
freedom!!!

(Joel 1:14-15, 2 Corinthians 3:17)

# REVELATION

Thank You that this will be a generation to seek
after Your heart, that will know the truth and
that the truth will set them free!  Thank You that
You are revealing Yourself to them and that
Your heart is being made known.  Jesus we pray
that not one would forget what You did on the
cross for them; do not let the enemy steal the
seed.  Send people to help cultivate the soil, so
that the seed would remain in good ground.
Come Lord Jesus, Come!

(2 Corinthians 3:17)

## CALLING

Jesus, thank You that You have called out each one of these youth by name and even if they feel too young, You say to them, "Do not say, 'I am only a youth', for to all to whom I send you, you shall go, and whatever I command you, you shall speak. Do not be afraid of them." Let this generation know Your truth and submit to Your word instead of what the world says.

(Jeremiah 1:4-10)

# COMING OUT

Abba, we declare and decree that this is the
generation that will be set apart for You; a
chosen generation, a holy nation, a royal
priesthood, a peculiar people. Abba we are
asking that You would set them so on fire for
You that without fear or hesitation they will
proclaim Your praises! God You are the One
who calls them out of darkness and into Your
marvelous light, so we decree a calling out right
now! Come out of the wickedness and
dissipation and know the King! Abba would
You call them forth to know You in
righteousness and holiness, to see the beauty of
the King and never look back from chasing after
You!

(1 Peter 2:9)

## LIFE

Jesus, thank You that You are raising up the youth as an exceedingly great army.  Let Your breath fill them and give them life, that wherever they go and in everything they do, You will flow out of them.  Abba, we ask that You would heal wounds in their hearts, so that they can live again.  Thank You that they are not a little army, but an exceedingly great one!  Holy Spirit fill them, so that they can truly live.

(Ezekiel 37:10,14)

# WARRIORS

God raise up a group of warriors that will love You so well that it will cause the whole world to look and see what You are doing, and would cause those all around them to acknowledge that You are God! Train them for battle and gird their loins with armor. May they wear the full armor of God to be able to fight well. God, we declare that the greatest weapons of their warfare is love combined with the Word for a magnificent double edged sword. Holy Spirit please teach them how to forgive, repent and overcome all of the obstacles thrown at them. May their lives give You great glory! In the mighty name of Jesus, Amen!

(Ephesians 6:10-17)

## GRACE

Lord, protect the ears of the youth. Lord protect their eyes. Keep their eyes from seeing the things that so grieve Your heart. Give them the grace to say no to ungodliness. We pray that they would set no worthless things before their eyes; that they would hate the work of those who fall away and it would not cling to them. Open their eyes, that they may behold the wonderful things from Your law. Please protect this generation from pornography and sexual immorality. Jesus, have mercy on those who have looked on it and protect those who have not. We ask for your abundant mercy O God, protect them and give them a hope which they can hold onto. Open their eyes to see what is wrong and draw them to Your heart, that all else will pass away. In Your holy name, AMEN!

(Psalm 119:18, Psalm 101:3)

# BEREAN CALL

Abba, raise up the youth who will know Your
word, who will recognize the power and
authority of it and who are equipped with Your
armor to fight Your battles well. Let them be
faithful Bereans who will receive the word with
gladness and then search out the Scriptures daily
to see if it is so. Abba, let them be ones who will
study to show themselves approved to God,
workmen who do not need to be ashamed, but
who rightly divide the Word of truth.

(Acts 17:11, 2 Timothy 2:15)

# HOLY ARMY

Lord we see an army coming together that will take out the forces of evil in this area. Abba could this generation of youth have what it takes to be that holy army? LORD could they be the ones who run after You and cause Your heart to skip a beat? We pray they are. Let Your word not pass us by again. We pray that we will not fail You, Great King. However, we do acknowledge that it is not by our strength, power or might, but by Your Spirit LORD. Father we desire to fulfill the mandate for this region, but also have come to realize that we cannot do it alone and that You are looking for a generation of youth who will fully be a part of starting, leading and stewarding it. May Your will be done in this region according to Your word, O God.

(Zechariah 4:6, Matthew 6:10)

# THANKSGIVING

Thank You Jesus that this is just the beginning of a radical life being possessed by the King of kings, who is love and life and holiness and truth! Thank You, that the good work that you have begun in each of the youth, You will complete until the day of Jesus Christ.

(Philippians 1:6)

## HOPE & GRACE

Jesus we thank You that You are giving the youth HOPE!  Jesus we ask that You stir a hope in each youth that they will be like You, because anyone who has this hope purifies himself!  Thank You, Jesus, that each one will purify himself, O God!  Abba, thank You for Titus 2:12 grace!  We ask that the youth will be taught the ability to say, "No" to ungodliness and worldliness and to live a self-controlled, upright and godly life in this present age, waiting for our blessed hope- the appearing of the glory of our God and Saviour Jesus Christ; You who gave Yourself to redeem us from all lawlessness, and to purify Yourself a people for Your very own possession who will be zealous for good works!  Come Lord Jesus come.

(Exodus 34:6-7, 1 John 3:2-3, Titus 2:11-14, Revelation 22:20, Judges 6:12)

# THE BRIDE

Father we decree that this is a generation that will hear the trumpet blown in Zion! Father we decree that this is a generation that will come before You with weeping and mourning and fasting and praying and sanctifying themselves, consecrating themselves to You and will come to You with everything!!! We decree that in this generation, mamby-pamby, half-hearted Christianity stops! We decree that this is a generation of all or nothing! We decree that the world has zero hold on them as they pursue after You. We decree that they will not fear man who is but a breath, but will fear You. We decree that the only thing that will matter to them is the King and His Kingdom! We decree that these are ones who will see the Holy Spirit poured out like never before. We decree over them that they will prophesy, and dream dreams; see visions, and receive the Holy Spirit like no generation before. We decree that the masses will call on the name of the Lord and be saved. Abba would You burn in their bones. We decree that Your truth will be powerfully proclaimed to every tribe and tongue and nation. Abba may they be the ones who look for Your return, calling out with the Spirit, "Come Lord Jesus, come!!!" Father we are pressing in for an outpouring on the young people like never seen before. Draw them O God.

(Joel 2:12-32, Jeremiah 20:9, Revelation 22:17-20, Revelation 19:7-9, Ephesians 5:27)

# HUNGER & THIRST

Father, we ask that this would be a generation that would not labour for the food which perishes, but would labour for the food which endures to everlasting life, which the Son of Man will give!  Father, we ask for youth to arise who would truly work the works of God, which is to believe on Jesus!  Jesus, we ask that each one would have complete revelation of who You are!  Jesus, You are the Bread of Life!  Father, may they know You, and believe in You.  Jesus, You said that he who feeds on You will live because of You, so we ask for a deep hunger in the youth to search You out and feed on You, and live forever because they are eating of You!  Jesus, You said clearly that no one can come to You unless the Father draws him, so Father we ask that You would draw each one right now!  Teach them Your ways.  Jesus, the youth are so longing for something that lasts forever, so would You open their hearts to hear You say, "I AM".  May they come to You and never hunger, and may they believe in You, and never ever thirst.  Father, we ask that even their whole households will eat of You.  Raise them up, O God.  Encourage their hearts to keep fighting and not to give up on their families.  You are good, Lord Jesus!!!

(John 6:27-29, John 6:35, John 6:44)

# AMBASSADORS

Jesus, call the youth.  Mark them.  We declare in Jesus' name that the youth of this generation are marked and chosen.  Thrust them out into Your harvest field.  Let them bring in the harvest for the glory of Your name.  Jesus, give them the faith of Bartimaeus; ones who will hear You coming and cry out and seek You out until they receive of You what they are longing for.  Jesus, when many rebuke them and tell them to be silent, let these youth be ones who will cry out the name of Jesus even louder.  Jesus, this generation will not quit; they will not be silenced!  They will declare Your name, Your praise, Your works, Your love, Your salvation, Your gospel all the louder for ALL the world to hear!!!  Jesus would You encounter them that they will fall on their faces before Your holiness and see You in all Your splendor and be wrecked for eternity.  Let these be ones who are compelled by the love of Jesus.  Let them know the fear of the Lord.  We declare that the love of Christ compels them, because they have concluded this, "That One has died for all, therefore all have died; and He died for all, that those who live might no longer live for themselves, but for Him who for their sake died and was raised."  God would these be ones that You could entrust the message of reconciliation to.  Therefore, let them be ambassadors for Christ, that You, God, would make Your appeal through these ones.  Let them implore others on Christ's behalf to be reconciled to God, because for their sake the Father made Jesus to be sin

DAY 19

who knew no sin, so that in You, Jesus, these youth might become the righteousness of God. We declare over them, "You are chosen to be the righteousness of God in Christ Jesus! In Jesus the old man has gone, the new has come!" Jesus, let Your love completely control and possess these lovers of the King that all they can do and pour out and speak and think and sing about is Love! You are love! Wreck them Jesus! Wreck them with Your love that they will never be the same again because they have encountered the living God and there is no turning back! All for the King! Let them be the ones who cry out, "Send me! I will go!!! Send me, Lord! I will go!"

(2 Corinthians 5:11-21, Mark 10:46-52, Isaiah 6:8, Matthew 9:38, 2 Corinthians 5:17)

# LIFE

Father we ask that this would be a generation
who would see the sins of their fathers and not
do likewise. Father may they be ones who are
given to You, who have not indulged in things
that grieve You, nor looked at idols, nor walked
in adultery and defilement. Father may they be
ones who bless others, giving abundantly of what
You have given them, lending without expecting
anything back. Abba we ask that they would be
ones who would gladly give their bread to the
hungry and clothing to the poor. Abba may they
be ones who treat the poor with justice and
execute Your judgments and walk in Your
statutes. Father thank You that You promise
that these ones will not die for the sin of their
fathers, but they shall surely live! We decree life
over this generation! Abba we ask that they
would clearly see the two ways set before them-
the way of life and the way of death- and that
they would choose You- the Way, the Truth and
the Life. Father may they choose life, so that
they may love You and obey Your voice and
cling to You, for You are their life and the
length of their days. May they dwell in the land
and destiny that You have purposed for them!

(Ezekiel 18:14-17, Deuteronomy 30:19-20, John 14:6)

DAY 20

# ARISE

Rise up, chosen warriors of the King!  Rise up, watchmen on the wall!  Rise up, youth!  Jesus, raise up the youth to sound the trumpet.  Open their eyes to hate the yuck and filth all around them.  Let them no longer call good evil and evil good, in Jesus' name.  God we ask for such a holy fear of God in the youth that would compel them to forsake all evil and pursue righteousness, holiness and purity.  Just as You are holy, Abba, let them be holy in all that they do, knowing that they were ransomed from the futile ways inherited from their forefathers, not with perishable things such as silver or gold, but with the precious blood of Christ, like that of a lamb without blemish or spot.

(1 Peter 1:15, Isaiah 5:20, Ezekiel 33:6, Joel 2:21, 2 Timothy 2:22)

# GRACE

We declare grace and peace to the youth.  We
praise You God and Father of our Lord Jesus
Christ, who has blessed the youth in Christ with
every spiritual blessing in the heavens.  For You,
O God, chose the youth of this generation before
the foundation of the world, to be holy and
blameless in Your sight.  In love, God, You
predestined them to be adopted through Jesus
Christ for Yourself, according to Your favour
and good will, to the praise of Your glorious
grace.  Jesus You created a path of redemption
for the youth in You, through Your blood that
was shed for them, the forgiveness of their
tresspasses, according to the riches of Your
grace that You lavished on them with all wisdom
and  understanding.  You are making known to
the youth of this hour the mystery of Your will,
according to Your good pleasure that You
planned in Christ Jesus for the administration of
the days of fulfillment.  LORD we ask that You
reveal to the youth that when they heard the
message of truth, the gospel of their salvation,
and when they believed in Jesus, they were
sealed with the promised Holy Spirit.  Thank
You God that Your Spirit is the down payment
of the youth's inheritance, for redemption of His
possession, to the praise of Your glory!  Amen.

(Ephesians 1:2-14)

# TRIUMPHANT

DAY 23

O Heavenly Father!  How You so love the children!!!  Father, we pray that the lives of these youth would give You glory.  Holy Father, please keep them safe by the power of Your name, the name that You gave Jesus, so that they may be unified with You.  Jesus, please watch over them, so that they will not be lost, but found.  We declare that this generation will have the same joy that Jesus has.  We declare that the youth will carry Your message to the ends of the earth and proclaim the goodness, mercy and grace of God.  LORD, we know that the world hates all those who belong to You.  We pray that each one will be strengthened with love, so that their hearts will not grow cold in these last days.  Protect them from the evil one.  LORD, let Your truth make them holy- Your words are truth.  May they be sent into the world just as Jesus was sent into the world.  Jesus, thank You for praying for every single one of them and interceding for them continually.  We declare the victory of the cross over their lives and pray that they will know Your power, glory, grace and love.  We cry out for these young men and women to see the truth, which will set them free.  We pray that You would liberate them and draw them to Yourself.  In the Mighty and Glorious Name of Jesus, Amen.

(John 17:10-19)

# UNASHAMED

Abba may this be a generation who loves the
praise of God more than the praise of man.
Father may they not only believe You, but
confess You publicly, no matter what the cost of
following You might be.  Jesus You already said
it costs everything, so we ask that the youth
would give You everything with great joy!
Father we ask that even if they are put out of the
churches that they would still love You and
confess who You really are.  Father regardless of
how sinful and adulterous this generation
becomes, may the youth be ones who stand
unashamedly in Your standard of holiness.
Jesus may they boldly confess You before men,
affirming that they are one with You.  Thank
You Jesus that as they see You, they see the
Father.  Jesus thank You that You came as a
light in the world, so that the youth can believe in
You and no longer abide in darkness.  Father we
ask that they would be ones who hear Your
words and believe them.

(John 12:42-50, Mark 8:38, Matthew 10:32)

## DESIRE

Jesus would You radically encounter the youth.
Jesus we pray that You would put a desire in
each of them to long after You and desire to
worship You in Spirit and in truth.  We pray they
would want to take Your yoke upon them and
learn from You, for You are gentle and humble
in heart, that each one of the youth would find
rest for their souls.  Jesus Your yoke is easy and
Your burden is light.

(Matthew 11:28-30, Ephesians 2:8-9, John 4:23-24)

# EKBALLO

Jesus ekballo (thrust forth) Your sons and daughters to find the youth who have been rejected by churches because of the gift of God that they carry. Show the youth others who carry Your gifts in their generation. Help them to seek out those who are willing to believe You, but do not know who You are yet, but will know You on account of the youth's testimony of You. Jesus please speak to them by Your Spirit, in dreams and visions and yes, LORD, even face to face encounters with You. Jesus we are crying out for this generation to have hearts that will believe and worship You in Spirit and in truth! Jesus You came into this world, so that those who do not see will see and those who do see will be blind. Then those who truly love You will be distinguishable from those who do not love You, but live in hypocrisy and self righteousness rather than the righteousness of God! LORD help the bride to purify herself, so that she can endure the day of Your coming and be able to stand when You appear, for You will be like a refiner's fire and like a cleansing lye. You will purify this generation and then they will come before You in righteousness and the offerings of their lives will please You as in the days of old and years gone by.

(John 9:35-39, Malachi 3:1-4)

# MOVE OF GOD

Jesus we lift up the youth and ask that You would set them on the path of righteousness. Jesus would You rise up the true church, so they can see You in us! Let Your Kingdom come. Jesus we ask that You would even begin to restore hope and show them that it is possible for things to change. Grow in them the character and hope needed to sustain this move of God. Jesus, thank You for divine strategies and grassroots movements that will be birthed out of the high schools and the youth. Would You download battle plans, even dreams, so that they would be encouraged that they are hearing Your voice! We lift up every youth and ask that this movement would be bigger than themselves. Give them the strength to be able to walk it out in excellence. Give them the hope and the courage to fight the good fight of faith to see Your Kingdom come here on earth as it is in heaven! Let the youth have a rhema word that they can hold on to, to carry them through the trials in Jesus' name! May they not grow wearying in doing good but set an example for the believers! Amen.

(Judges 7:9-15, Galatians 6:9-10, Proverbs 3:6, Proverbs 4:11-13, Romans 5:3-5, John 10:27, Proverbs 20:29, 1 Timothy 6:12, Matthew 6:10, James 1:2-4)

DAY 27

# LOVE

Jesus, we praise You for calling this generation
out of darkness and into Your marvelous light.
Thank You that You have called each one of
these for such as time as this. You purposed
them to be alive right here, right now. Jesus,
would You call them out from being orphans to
being the ones who will go boldly before Your
throne to intercede on behalf of their people and
their generation. Call them out as the Esthers,
as kings and priests before You. Let them be
ones who will lay down their lives to see the
deliverance and salvation of their generation,
because they were willing to risk their own lives
for others. May they know that the greatest act
of love is that a man lay down his life for his
friends. O' Jesus, would You do it in them.
Would You begin to grow that love in them now.
For the glory of Your name, Jesus.

(1 Peter 2:9, Esther 2:5, Esther 2:8, 1 John 15:13)

# MINISTER

Jesus, thank You that You are raising up a new generation who will be like the Levitical priests who were the descendants of Zadok and who guarded Your sanctuary while the Israelites went astray from You. We pray that they would come near to minister before You, and that they would stand before You to offer sacrifices of obedience. LORD, may each youth enter Your sanctuary, that they alone would come near Your table to minister before You and serve You as guards. When they enter the gates of Your inner court, may they clothe themselves in the compassion, kindness, humility, gentleness, and patience you have called them to, so they can continually minister to You day and night! Rise up a generation that would call You HOLY and walk in Your holiness. In Jesus' name, AMEN!

(Ezekiel 44:15-17, 1 Samuel 15:22, Colossians 3:12, 1 Peter 1:16)

# FIRE

Raise up the youth Lord!  Raise them up!  Set a
fire in them that they can't contain that they
can't control.  Let them desire You in a
passionate way that they never have before.
Raise them up!  Thank You for ekballoing them
into the labour field!  Thank You that they are
beginning to be faithful and are beginning to
pursue You. Draw them Lord, so that they may
come to You.  Papa, reveal Your nature to them;
reveal Your truth and Your love, so that they can
know for themselves who YOU are!  Transform
them with the power of Your Holy Spirit.
Reveal the deep hidden things of God.

(John 6:44, Matthew 9:38)

# LIFE

Breathe on these dry bones O God!!! Abba would You let Your breath come and blow through the youth, blow through the schools and raise up a mighty army for Your kingdom and for Your glory! Be glorified O God! Abba, give the youth wisdom and courage to prophesy as You command, so that life can come! We prophesy to these bones and say, "O dry bones, hear the word of the Lord. Surely God will cause breath to enter into you, and you shall live. He will put sinews on you and bring flesh upon you and cover you with skin and put breath in you and you shall live. Then you shall know that He is the Lord." Abba, let us continue to prophesy and press in until life comes into the body! So we prophesy again and say to the breath, "Thus says the Lord God, 'Come from the four winds O breath, and breathe on these slain that they may live.'" Abba, we thank You for the life coming now and the youth standing to their feet; an exceedingly great army.

(Ezekiel 37:5-9)

## SEEK

Abba, raise up a people who will believe that
You have a purpose for them and will run after
You! Let them be ones who seek You with all of
their heart until they truly find You; to know
You so well that they can bring a generation with
them! Abba, would you restore our young
people and gather them from the darkness and
depravity to which they have been
scattered. Draw them to Your heart O God!

(Jeremiah 29:11-13)

## ARISE

Abba, we thank You that You are raising up an
army of youth for praise and renown among all
the people. Thank You that You are singing
Your song of victory over them and that You are
gathering the outcasts and calling those who
mourn to Your festival.

(Zephaniah 3:16-20)

# SEEK

Jesus, we thank You for a generation who is seeking after You! We declare a hunger over them to seek You until they find You! Jesus, You promise that if they seek You with all of their hearts they will find You!

(Jeremiah 29:12-14)

# FIRE

Jesus, set the youth ablaze. God, You have had this plan and purpose long before we were born. Set Your holy fire on the youth that will cause them to fervently and passionately pursue You. LORD, set eternity in their hearts that they would live beyond what this life offers and not chase after dust their whole lives. Help them to see that You are their greatest treasure and second to You is people. Help them to love extravagantly and compel them to turn from wickedness. Purge all filth and bloodshed from their midst by Your Spirit of Judgment and Fire, knowing Your judgments are good and just. Holy Spirit please teach them how to pray and pursue the heart of the Father. Amen.

(Isaiah 4:4, Luke 3:16-17)

# REVIVAL

Jesus, do what it takes to set the youth ablaze for You! Let them know they are loved while You prepare and refine them! Jesus we thank You, and we trust that You will rise up a people who will love You with everything they are! Jesus, thank You that You have woken them from the way they were living. God, would You continue to draw them to Your heart, as none can come unless You draw them! Jesus, may they not forget what You have done in their lives. Continue to shake them until they arise to see Your kingdom come! Let them not fall back asleep!!! Let them rest in Your arms. May they abide in the shadow of Your wings. Thank You that You have not left them nor forsaken them, and that You are calling them out of the darkness and into a marvelous light to proclaim your goodness. God let them not forget what You have done and let conversations even begin at school about You. May others hear the good works You have done. Let them run with the gospel, O God! Thank You for rising up another generation that *will not* let Your presence pass by them. Thank You for those who are faithfully praying! Continue to send others. May they be one as we are ONE!!! We pray for great faith to come into the schools. Would You repeat the revival that you did at Woodlawn here. Let the schools come together and make history. Don't let us hold You back; reckless abandonment is what we need! Let Your Spirit come and hover over the school as You did with the Israelites! Encounter the principals!!! Encounter the teachers and the assistants. May they see what You are doing and give glory to You God! We pray for Your mercy on those who may try and oppose the move of God. We pray that You would begin drawing them to Your heart right now, and forgive them for they do not know what they do. Let this be the revival that is talked about in the history books and has been shared time and time again through prophecies. Let it not pass by us, O God; let it not pass by us. Let us know what will hinder the move of God and how we can remove the obstacles. Give the youth wisdom and understanding, in Jesus' name! Thank you Jesus! Amen.

(Matthew 22:37, John 6:44, Hebrews 13:5, Psalm 91:1, 1 Peter 2:9, Mark 3:25)

# NEW CREATION

Abba, we ask that You would reveal the gospel
to the youth in its fullness and truth.  You are
truth Jesus.  Holy Spirit, lead them into all
truth.  Show them the power of the cross, that
the cry of their hearts and the heart of this
generation would be, "That I may know nothing
but Christ and Him crucified."  Let it be their
resolve to know nothing but You Jesus and You
crucified.  Crucify them on the cross with you, O
God, and make them new; that it is no longer
they who live, but Christ who lives in them and
that the life that they now live in the flesh they
live by faith in the Son of God who loved them
and gave Himself for them.  Let them live out of
the fullness of what You did for them!

(John 16:13, 1 Corinthians 2:2, Galatians 2:20)

## ARISE

Raise up the youth O God! Let them be a
generation fully given to You and fully laid
down. Let them be the ones who are willing to
sell everything that they have to buy the field and
gain the kingdom.

(Matthew 13:44)

# FAITH

We rebuke all doubt in the youth in Jesus'
name. Please help them in their unbelief. We
speak forth the realness of God and the truth of
who You are. Holy Spirit we ask that You
manifest Yourself to them beyond human
reasoning and logic. LORD, may they
understand who You have created them to be
and the destiny You have for them in this
generation. We call forth the warriors and sons
and daughters to the forefront of this
generation.

(Mark 9:24)

## AWAKENING

Abba, we thank You that You can do more than
we could even ask or imagine. Thank You that
this is possible. Thank You that our
communities will see that next great awakening
through the youth. Let it come!

(Luke 9:32)

## OBEDIENCE

Abba, thank You that You are raising up youth
whose hands are trained for war and their fingers
for battle. Thank You Jesus that You are raising
up an army that will hear Your voice so clearly
that even if You tell them to wait until they hear
the sound of marching in the treetops, they will
obey and not move until You do and will defeat
the enemy. Let this be a generation of radical
obedience. Jesus, we pray that the fear of God
would so come upon these youth that they will
not be able to do anything but obey You,
because they know You- Your greatness,
holiness, love and power. Thank You Jesus for
lives laid down. It is these who are not defiling
themselves with lust. It is these who follow the
Lamb wherever he goes. These have been
redeemed from mankind as first fruits for God
and the Lamb. Let Your kingdom come in this
generation; let it come in us!

(Psalm 144:1, 2 Samuel 5:24, Revelation 14:4)

DAY 41

## PROTECTION

Jesus, we pray that the youth would not drink the
maddening wine of sexual immorality, but rather
would hunger and thirst for righteousness. With
a world searching to fill the gap hole in their
lives- Jesus You already are the gap filler- may
they be filled with the knowledge of who You are
and tangibly experience Your presence, so that
they would no longer desire the immorality of
the world! Jesus protect the youth from
pornography and begin to set up leaders who will
take this mantle and fight! In Jesus' name,
amen!

(Revelation 18:3-4)

# MIND OF CHRIST

Jesus, thank You for a generation of youth rising
up who will be with You where you are, who will
follow the Lamb wherever He goes, who will lay
down their lives and not love their lives to death,
and who will pick up their cross and follow
You.  May they have this mind among
themselves, which is theirs in Christ Jesus, who,
though He was in the form of God, did not count
equality with God a thing to be grasped, but
emptied Himself by taking the form of a servant
being born in the likeness of men.  And being
found in human form, He humbled Himself by
becoming obedient to the point of death, even
death on a cross.  Therefore, God You highly
exalted Him and bestowed on Him the name
that is above every name.  At the mention of
Jesus every knee will bow, in heaven and on
earth and under the earth and every tongue
confess that Jesus Christ is Lord, to the glory of
God the Father.  May the youth do all things
without grumbling or disputing that they may be
blameless and innocent, children of God without
blemish in the midst of a crooked and twisted
generation, among whom they shine as lights in
the world, holding fast to the word of life.  Let
them be filled with Your same mind Jesus, of
love, humility, compassion and faith, and let
them be blameless and innocent children of God,
who shine as lights in the world and to hold fast
to the words of life.

(Philippians 2:5-11, Philippians 2:14-16)

# ARISE

Jesus, we ask that You would raise up a people
of purity before You.  Would You raise up these
youth as ones who are not hypocritical, but see
You for who You really are and make a clear
decision either for or against You, not in the
middle.  Let them be the ones who see You
because of their purity of heart!  Let them be the
ones who fully say yes to You, not with lip
service, but as ones who are truly given to You,
fervently serving the Lord!  Abba, let Your
kingdom come upon them.  We declare that they
are a people to show forth Your praises; a
people who will love You so well that Your
kingdom can come in them, through them and
all around them; that they will be the generation
who will not be afraid to pursue You, but will see
the greater things than these as they give
themselves COMPLETELY to You! Jesus You
have begun a good work and thank You that
You are completely faithful to complete it!  In
Jesus' name!

(Matthew 5:8, Ephesians 6:6)

# FIRE

FIRE! FIRE! FIRE! HOLY SPIRIT FIRE!
Holy all consuming fire come upon the youth
and their families today LORD. Baptize the
youth with Your fire Holy Spirit and fill them
with Your presence in Jesus Name.

(Hebrews 12:29)

## CALLED

Jesus, we thank You for each youth You have called into Your house. Jesus we thank You for You have called them for such a time as this to fight for their loved ones. Lord, would You show them who they really are, yet keep them hidden until the time necessary for them to be revealed. Raise up a loyalty like You have never seen before! May they be willing to go anywhere to see Your Kingdom come!

(Ruth 1:15-18, Esther 4:14)

# GRACE

LORD, Your glory is on the youth. Jesus, in Your mercy please show us how we can help them become all that You have created them to be. LORD, we pray that You would fill each of them with Your wisdom and teach them to pray and love beyond measure. We pray for an acceleration in grace! LORD, we pray that sin would be a stench in their nostrils and they would be able to distinguish between what is You and what is not and that they would make You the clear choice. Lord save them and baptize them with Your fire!

(Hebrews 5:14, Joshua 24:14-15)

DAY 47

## SURRENDERED

Possess the youth Abba. Take over. Let them be
ones who will take the plunge and surrender all,
holding nothing back. Spirit of Truth, guide
them in all truth that they will know the power of
the gospel and not doubt. We ask that You
would remove all attraction to the things of the
world, that all they would long for is You.
Would You be the one thing that they desire and
are longing for, their one satisfaction, their one
goal. Let all else fade in the light of Your
presence. Let them behold Your beauty Jesus.

(John 16:13, Psalm 27:4)

## OVERCOME

It's not by might nor by power; it's by Your
Spirit! Jesus, we thank You that the mountains
that are needing to be overcome are nothing for
You! Where the youth think it's impossible,
Lord we agree that by Your Spirit it IS
possible!!! Thank you God, that You are a God
of the impossible. Thank You Lord!

(Zechariah 4:6, Luke 18:27)

## REVELATION

Abba, would You show the youth the power of
Your love and gospel, that they would count
everything else, everything of this world as dung,
that they may win Christ and be found in You,
knowing they do not  have their own
righteousness, which is of the law, but that which
is of faith in the Christ, the righteousness which
is of God through faith.  Abba, would You let
them know You and the power of Your
resurrection and the fellowship of Your
sufferings that they would be made like You in
Your death.  Let them count everything as loss
for the surpassing knowledge of Jesus Christ.
Abba, let them press on that they may attain
unto the resurrection of the dead.  That they may
be one with You, Jesus.

(Philippians 3:7-12)

# GRACE

Jesus, we pray that the youth would begin to hunger for Your righteousness and grace! Jesus, we pray that You would give them the grace to turn away from ungodly movies, games and music, and to begin seeking Your heart on these issues. Lord, would they be ones to fill their lives with the purity and hope in which You have called them! Thank You for the supernatural grace You have given to many of the youth to not want to watch the movies that grieve Your heart; may it be so with the youth in this region. Thank You for Your faithfulness in calling each one of them. Thank You that You will do it!

(Ephesians 2:8-9)

# GRACE

Daddy, would you raise up this generation as the
ones who truly will say no to ungodliness and
worldly passions and live soberly, righteously and
godly in this present age.  Abba, would you pour
out Your grace upon them so that they might
know you!  Set them on fire.  Jesus, we are
asking for a young generation full of grace, who
will so know You that they will see things the
way You see them and have zero desire for the
immorality that is so prevalent in our nation.
Abba, raise up a people holy and righteous.  Let
them be the forerunners of young men and
women committed and empowered in purity.
We cry, "Come out of perversion!"  We call forth
a generation, pure and spotless before the
Lord!

(Titus 2:11)

# HOLINESS

Jesus, thank You for the youth. Let them know the power of the cross. Jesus, who You set free will be free indeed. Raise up a generation of youth who will be pure and holy and not be tainted by sexual immorality, but will be truly free and walk with the Lamb wherever He goes; who will not defile themselves with lust and who will not love their lives to death, O God, but they will have the greatest love- laying down their lives for their brothers!

(John 8:36, Revelation 14:4, Revelation 12:11, John 15:13)

## CAUSE

Jesus, let this people be consumed by the cause of Christ.  Is there not a cause?  We declare over the youth that there is a cause for living, there is a cause for fighting, there is a cause for pressing in past our comfort and seeing others set free. There is a cause and it is seeking after You and bringing You great glory.  Jesus, would You burn a cause in the hearts of each of these young people that Your desire for them would become their desire and that You would be honoured and glorified.  Let them be a part of the people you have been looking for!

(1 Samuel 17:29)

## NEW HEART

Holy Spirit, You are the great Teacher. Please
teach the youth Your ways, so that they may
know You. Please reveal Your great love to
them as You passionately pursue them. Show
them Your heart and create in them a new heart
O God; a heart that can perceive you!

(John 14:26)

## PRAYER

God, we thank You that when we don't know what to pray, Holy Spirit You will show us what we ought to pray. Thank You that You can do the same with the youth. We pray that You would continue to lead them into intercession while they come to your throne boldly. Jesus, we pray they will be able to deal with their stuff quickly, so their hearts won't grow cold in this season. Protect each one You have called and pursue them with Your love. In Jesus name, amen!

(Romans 8:26)

# OPEN HEART

Thank You Jesus for what You are teaching the
youth in this season.  Jesus, we pray that You
would open their hearts wide to receive Your
message that You have for them.  Let them not
forget what You are trying to teach them, rather,
they would store up Your word in their hearts
that they may not sin against You.  Thank You
for the revelation You pour out to Your children
and that You are a good Dad who gives good
gifts and wants the best for them.  As they
receive Your word, let it be in good soil so that it
will not be choked, stolen, or dried out.  We pray
for a softening of the heart right now, a hunger
for Your word to come and that it would be
deeply rooted.  Let the watchman on the wall
know how and when to pray, so that we could
ward off the enemy trying to sow weeds.  Thank
You for calling the youth to pray, so that Your
glory will be made known and that Your
Kingdom will come!  In Jesus name we pray,
Amen!!!

(Acts 16:14, Psalm 119:11, Matthew 13:1-30)

## CALLING

Jesus, would You raise up the youth as ones who will prepare a way before You and make a straight path for You to come and enter their school, their homes and their lives.  Jesus, let them be ones who lay down their all at Your feet, recognizing that You are the one who is mighty and worthy of it all and it is their greatest joy to minister to You.  Abba, would You baptize them with the Holy Spirit and fire!  Call them out, O God.  Let them be ones who are not afraid to be different in order to obey and represent You.  Jesus, let them see and desire You.  We ask that You would burn in their hearts and draw them, so they can say yes to You, so You can do what You have been longing to do in this area.  Put a yes cry in their hearts, O God!  We love You Jesus!

(Mark 1:2-3, Mark 1:7, Mark 7:8, Matthew 3:11)

# NEW CREATION

Thank You, Jesus that You have not given the youth a spirit of timidity or fear, but You have given them the Spirit of power, love and a sound mind. Renew their minds in You, Lord, that they put off the old man and put on the new man which is created according to God in true righteousness and holiness.

(1 Timothy 1:7, Ephesians 4:22-24)

# WARRIOR

Jesus, thank You for each and every one of the
youth.  Thank You that You have marked them
for Yourself.  Let them see that they have been
marked and not be afraid and run from You, but
be bold and seek after You all the more.  Would
You cause them to hunger and thirst for
righteousness that they might be filled and
satisfied by Your goodness.  Jesus, let them hear
You knocking, so that they will open the door
and dine with You and You with them.  Thank
You, Jesus.  Let them be bold like Joshua and
take the ground that You have given them that
the whole land might be won for the King of
kings.  Let them not be afraid to fight the giants,
but would You first train them with the lions and
the bears that when the giants arise,  they will
know their God and they will have the faith in
You to overcome Goliath.  Close their ears to
those who try to discourage them and tell them
that they are too young, untrained, unqualified
or proud.  Give them the boldness and righteous
anger like David to see ungodliness and injustice
die in the land.  Thank You, Jesus.  Thank You
that this generation of youth are not quitters, but
overcomers!  Amen.

(Joshua 1:9, 1 Samuel 17)

# OVERCOMER

Through You God, the youth will push back against the darkness; through Your name, Jesus, they will trample down wickedness that tries to rise up against them. LORD You are their strength and their shield. May their hearts trust in You, because we know LORD, that You will help them. Therefore, may their hearts exult You with singing and dancing. May they thank You God for all that You are doing in, through and around them.

(Psalm 28:7, Psalm 44:5)

## THANKSGIVING

Thank You Lord for You have been good to each one of the youth. Help them remember what You have done for them. Let them not forget Your benefits. You will heal all their diseases and forgive all of their iniquities. Help them to see Your beauty and give You thanks. May You be honoured and glorified O God. In Jesus' name we pray, amen!!!

(Psalm 130:2)

# TRUST

Help the youth step out of the boat, even though it's stormy and the waves may seem high. Let them know that they can trust you with their lives; You will NEVER let them down. Thank You for the storms the youth are walking through and learning that can hold onto You and trust You at a deeper level. Let them all get out of the boat and press on toward the prize that is worth far more than gold!!!

(Matthew 14:22-33)

## ARISE

Jesus, thank You that You are choosing the
weak and the foolish in this world to confound
the minds of the wise and the strong.  Thank
You that when the youth have been looked down
on, despised and degraded by society, that they
will rise up a strong army who will set an
example for the believers in speech, life, love,
faith and purity.  Thank You that they will no
longer be thought of as insignificant, but You are
quickly rising them up.  Thank You that what
You are doing in the spirit is showing in the
natural in how our government is looking to hear
from the youth for solutions.  Thank You that
You are doing a new thing.  The ones that
society looked down on are now quickly rising to
leadership and they will confound the minds of
the wise.  Thank You Jesus.  Amen.

(1 Timothy 4:12, Isaiah 43:19)

# REPENTANCE

Father blow Your wind of revival over the
youth.  We pray that they would humble
themselves and pray, seek Your face and turn
from everything that  is wicked and grieves Your
heart knowing You are a forgiving and merciful
God who will hear them when they cry out and
will heal the brokenness around them.

(2 Chronicles 7:14)

# WISDOM

Abba, let the youth incline their ear to wisdom and apply their hearts to understanding. May they cry out for discernment and lift up their voices for understanding; that they would seek for her as for silver and search for her as for hidden treasure, so that then they will understand the fear of the Lord and find the knowledge of God. You are the God who gives wisdom and from Your mouth comes knowledge and understanding. Jesus, let them understand righteousness and justice, equity and every good path. Let wisdom enter their hearts and knowledge be pleasant to their souls. Let discretion preserve them and understanding keep them, to deliver them from the way of evil and from the man who speaks of perverse things, and from those who leave the paths of uprightness to walk in the ways of darkness. We pray that Wisdom would deliver them from the seductress who flatters with her words and who forsakes the companion of her youth and forgets the covenant of her God. May the youth walk in the way of goodness and keep to the paths of righteousness. For the upright youth will dwell in the land and the blameless will remain in it, but the wicked will be cut off from the earth and the unfaithful will be uprooted from it. Holy Spirit, let them go after You and leave everything else behind. Let them be pure before You, Father.

(Proverbs 2)

# STRATEGY

Abba, let the youth do what man says is impossible by simply being faithful in the little that You have asked of each of them. Father let them know Your heart and not be discouraged by the taunts of the enemy. Lord, if each one turns to You, then a whole generation will be saved! If each one builds their house, then the whole city will be saved! If each one turns his life around, then a whole school gets turned around. We say no to the discouragement of the enemy that says this generation is too far gone! This is a generation marked by the King! Chosen by the King! We declare over the youth, "Do not be afraid of them! Remember the Lord who is great and awesome and fight for your brothers, your sons, your daughters, your wives and your homes!" Daddy, thank You that You are frustrating the plan of the enemy! Jesus we ask for strategies from heaven for the youth to be able to build while protecting one another. Raise up those that You would have build and raise up those that You would have stand guard. Teach them how to build with one hand and hold their weapon with the other, so that no one gets taken out. Daddy, we ask that in the place where they hear Your trumpet sound, that they would rally together for their God will fight for them. Father, thank You for raising up a mighty army of ones who say yes! Give them the courage to say yes, O God!

(Nehemiah 4:14-20, Nehemiah 3)

## EYES TO SEE

We speak over the youth that they will behold
the One who forms mountains and creates the
wind and declares to man what His thoughts are;
He who makes dawn into darkness and treads on
the high places of the earth- The LORD God of
hosts is His name.  Jesus, Emmanuel!

(Amos 4:13)

# LABOURERS

Jesus, we thank you for each one of the
youth. Saturate their hearts with Your love, so
they will be compelled by love. Abba, send out
the labourers; ekballo the labourers, for the
harvest is ripe- the labourers are few. Open their
eyes to see and the ears to hear. May You be
honoured and glorified! Hallelujah! In Your
name it shall be done!

(Matthew 9:37-38, Luke 10:2)

## DEVOTED

Jesus, let the youth experience You and fall in love with You, never looking back! Let them cry out like David that You are the one thing they seek after; that they would long to dwell in Your house all their days, just to gaze at Your beauty and talk with You! Abba, would You stir up a yearning for You in them that they would cry out that one day in Your presence is better than thousands elsewhere.

(Psalm 27:4, Psalm 84:10)

# FREEDOM

Abba, we speak Your life over the youth. Let
them live in the fullness of You and Your
kingdom. Thank You that Your breath gives us
life Abba, so would You breathe Your life into
them. Show them the life and the light of the
gospel that they will truly live in Your freedom-
for whom the Son sets free is free indeed. Thank
You for the fullness of Your love flowing in and
through the youth that they will truly confound
the minds of the wise. Abba, let them so
radically encounter You and Your goodness that
like Moses they will never want to go anywhere
without You.

(Ephesians 3:19, Job 33:4, John 8:36,
1 Corinthians 1:27, Exodus 33:15)

## WISDOM

We declare that the youth in this region will not be slaves to sin, but will be mastered by righteousness; that they will fear the LORD and nothing else. This is the beginning of wisdom, and we pray for the gift of wisdom to fill each one powerfully and that they would be filled with grace to accomplish all that You have planned for them to fulfill.

(Romans 6:16, Proverbs 9:10, 1 Corinthians 12:8, 1 Peter 5:10)

# KINGDOM

Jesus, we pray Your kingdom come, Your will be
done in the youth, that no weapon formed
against them shall prosper, in Jesus' name.  May
Your name be glorified through the youth.  In
Jesus' name we pray, amen!

(Isaiah 54:17)

DEVOTED

# DEVOTED

DAY 74

We declare over the youth that EVERYTHING that they have counted gain, that it will now be counted as loss for Christ; that they will count all things loss for the excellence of the knowledge of Christ Jesus their Lord. In His name they will gladly suffer the loss of all things and count them as rubbish, that they may gain Christ and be found in Him, not having their own righteousness, from the law, but that which is through faith in Christ, the righteousness which is from God by faith. Jesus, we declare that they will be ones who know You and the power of Your resurrection and the fellowship of Your sufferings, being conformed to Your death; that they may attain to the resurrection from the dead. We declare a generation who will give everything to gain You.

(Philippians 3:7-11, Matthew 13:44)

## NOT SHAKEN

Jesus, we ask that You would train up an army of
youth who will not be shaken. No matter what
comes their way let them not be shaken, O God,
but let them be the ones who hear Your word
and do it, so that they build their house on the
solid Rock of Jesus. Let them be faithful
Bereans who will study the Scripture to see if
what they are hearing is true.

(Matthew 7:24-27, Acts 17:11)

## HOLINESS

O good and merciful God, please place a desire
in the youth to present their bodies a living and
holy sacrifice to You, acceptable to God, which
is their spiritual service of worship.  We speak
over them, "Do not be conformed to this world,
but be transformed by the renewing of your
mind, so that you may prove what the will of God
is, that which is good and acceptable and
perfect." In Jesus name, amen.

(Romans 12:1-2)

# GOD'S PLAN

Jesus, we thank You for this opportunity to be able to cry out to You on behalf of the youth. We pray that Your will would be done in each child's life. Thank You that You have a plan and purpose- plans to prosper them and not to harm them, plans of a hope and future, that when they seek You, they will find You!

(Jeremiah 29:11-12)

## DEVOTED

Jesus, we ask that You would encounter the youth. Father, give them a deep desire to know You and celebrate You. Jesus, would You give them a hate for the things that grieve You and take Your place and simply distract from celebrating You. Father, give them a desire to seek after You and You only, that You would have first place in their lives. Jesus, we ask for a generation without idolatry. Give them a hate for ALL idols and eyes to see them for what they are and then eyes to see You for who You really are- Glorious Jesus!!!

(Exodus 20:3)

# MOVE OF GOD

Father, would You shake all of the parents who
have encountered You in their past; are there
any left who still follow you?  Father, how will
they see this next great move of Yours?  Some
gave up hope on You coming powerfully!
LORD move on them.  Send Your messengers
to say to them and their children, "Now be
strong, O parents. And be strong, O youth, and
be strong all people, and work; for I am with you,
says the LORD of Hosts with the Word who cut
a covenant with you when He hung on the cross,
and the Spirit of God remains among
you."  LORD may they not fear when You shake
the heavens, and the earth, and the sea, and the
dry land.  You are going to shake all the nations
and the desire of all nations shall come and You
will fill Your house with glory.  The silver is
Yours and the gold is Yours.  Abba, You
promised that the glory of the latter house will
be greater than that of the former and we believe
You!  Please give them Your peace in this hour,
Amen.

(Haggai 2:3-9)

## HOLINESS

Call them out of sexual immorality, Jesus!  Let
the youth be Your pure and spotless bride that
You are coming back for.  Let them be the ones
who are ready and eagerly waiting for Your
return.  Let them be the ones who follow the
Lamb wherever He goes and do not love their
lives to death.   Let it no longer be they who live,
but Christ who lives in them.  The life that they
now live, they live by faith in the Son of God who
loves them and gave Himself for them.

(Revelation 19:8, Revelation 12:11, Galatians 2:20)

# CALLING

Jesus, would Your kingdom come upon the
youth; let Your glory be manifest in their
lives. Thank You for how You called each one
to rebuild the walls that have been torn down.
Teach them to fight while building Your
kingdom. Show them where they need to be and
what part of the body You have called them to,
so they may be able to choose to walk in the
calling You have for them. Jesus, we pray that
they would walk in Your ways and never depart
from You. Thank You that You will never leave
them nor forsake them and You are near to all
who call upon You; to all who call upon You in
truth. You will fulfill the desire of those who
fear You. You will also hear their cry and will
save them.

(Psalm 145:18-19)

# INTIMACY

Jesus, we ask for this generation of youth, that
they would be ones who say yes to You and go
out as labourers into the harvest. Jesus, we are
praying for You, the Lord of the Harvest, to
send out labourers!  Father, we ask that these
would be ones who say yes to You and see all
that You promised would happen as they go in
obedience to You.  Abba, we ask that they would
see the sick healed and the demons subject to
them in Your name.  We declare that they are
ones who will believe You for all authority to
trample on serpents and scorpions, for authority
over all the power of the enemy and for authority
that nothing will harm them.  But Father, even as
they believe You, we ask that they will be ones
who will not merely go after the signs and
wonders, but that their greatest joy will be that
their names are written in heaven, that they
belong to You and bring You glory and
pleasure.  We are praying that their greatest joy
will be intimacy with the King, and all that is
needed will be supplied.  In Jesus' name.

(Luke 10:2, Luke 10:17-20)

# REVIVAL

LORD, we thank You so much for each of the
youth who have been dancing, singing, playing,
worshiping and helping serve the community!
Jesus, we ask for a rich reward for them! May
they powerfully encounter You. Abba, You
know what it would take to start a revival in each
one and we are asking that You set their hearts
ablaze for You. God, that they would be filled
with supernatural grace, wisdom, power and
authority to do the good works that You have
planned in advance for them. God, we pray that
they would know the joy and excitement of
following You and the crazy adventures You
have planned for them!

(Ephesians 2:10)

## HOLINESS

Jesus, raise up a generation of youth who will not
conform to the world in any way, but will press
after You with everything they are. Let them
truly pursue holiness and the character of
Jesus. Thank You Jesus that Your cross made
the way for holiness before You. Mark Your
holy ones Abba. We ask that You would choose
these ones and many more.

(1 Peter 1:13-16)

## LOVE

Jesus, we ask that Your love would abound more and more in the youth, that they would clearly be able to approve what is good and hate what is evil, so that they would be pure and blameless when You come Jesus. Let them think on such things that are true, honest, just, pure, lovely, commendable, excellent and praiseworthy in Jesus' name. Abba, let their love be genuine. We pray they will abhor what is evil and cling to what is good.

(Philippians 1:9-11, Philippians 4:8, Romans 12:9)

DAY 85

# HUNGER

Jesus, would You raise up these youth to long for
You more than anything else.  Father, we ask
that You would put a desire in their hearts to
pursue You and love You more than anything.
Encounter them O, God.  Let them know
You.  Jesus, we know You desire that they would
know You and come to repentance, so Father we
ask that You would draw them and soften their
hearts towards You.  Would You put a cry in
their heart that would proclaim a day in Your
courts is better than a thousand anywhere else;
that they would rather be a doorkeeper in Your
house than to dwell in the tents of wickedness.
Father, would You let them taste of You, so that
they will hunger for You more than anything
else.  Thank You for those who have tasted of
You, and we ask that they would not quench the
hunger with other things that don't really satisfy,
but that instead they would run to You, the
bread of Life, to eat and never be hungry.

(Psalm 84:2, Psalm 84:10, John 6:35)

# TRUTH

Thank You Jesus for manifesting Yourself in
front of the youth in a display of Your great
love. Thank You for taking the time to reveal
Your nature and heart. You are amazing and
kind! Thank You for showing mercy to those
whom You choose to show mercy. We ask that
You would continue to show mercy and give
them grace at the same time. Especially in this
season with so many lies being tossed around, we
pray that You would reveal Your nature to them
and their family; Jesus You cannot lie. We ask
that they would be vessels of truth and hope!
Let them speak Your truth in school and let
Your Spirit come in that place, because where
the Spirit of the Lord is, there is freedom!

(2 Corinthians 3:17)

## PURPOSE

Jesus, we thank You for each one You have placed on our hearts to pray for. We pray that no weapon formed against them shall prosper in Jesus' name; that Your plan and purpose would be done in their lives. We pray Lord that You would soften their hearts and give them the grace to choose You. We pray that You would bless each one with the knowledge of You and that they would be filled with Your love because knowledge without love is no good. Let Your church be edified. In Jesus' name we pray, amen.

(Isaiah 54:17, 1 Corinthians 13:2)

# LOVE

Jesus, let the youth be filled to the fullest with
Your love that is patient and kind; Your love
that is not jealous or boastful, not arrogant or
rude; Your love that does not insist on its own
way; love that is not irritable or resentful.  Fill
them with Your love that does not rejoice in
iniquity, but rejoices in the truth; Your love that
bears all things, believes all things, hopes all
things and endures all things; Your love that
never fails.  Let it be Your love that is without
hypocrisy, that abhors what is evil and clings to
what is good.  Let them first be overcome by and
receive Your love for them and then be filled
with Your love to give out, first to You and then
to others.  Let it be a love that others recognize
as a love that comes only from Jesus.

(1 Corinthians 13:4-8, Romans 12:9, John 13:35)

DAY 89

# SEEK

Jesus, we declare that the youth are overcomers. Jesus, we ask that they would be ones who will seek You, Lord, while You may be found and call upon You while You are near. Father, we're asking that the wicked would forsake his way and the unrighteous his thoughts and God that they return to You. Father, let even the unrighteous thoughts be forsaken, so that they can find mercy and forgiveness in You! Jesus, would You lead them to repentance, so they can truly know You and be known by You. Jesus, would You place a deep, unrelenting desire in the youth to seek after You. Abba, let them seek You more than gold or silver, or jobs, careers, marriage or anything else in life. God, let them see that true purpose and calling is only found in You, even in suffering for doing what's right. Jesus, raise up a people who will not back down because of suffering, but will instead embrace it for the glory of Your name.

(Isaiah 55:6-7)

# SUFFERING

Abba, we pray that the youth would have a deep revelation that there is no credit if they have sinned and are treated harshly. However, reveal to them that when they do what is right and suffer for it and patiently endure it, that they will find favour with You! Abba, we pray that they will know and understand that this is the very thing that You have called them to since Jesus also suffered for them, leaving an example for each one to follow in His steps. Jesus You committed no sin, nor was any deceit found in Your mouth and while being reviled, Jesus You did not revile in return, so we pray that the youth will not revile. Jesus You did not threaten, so we declare that the youth will not threaten. And we declare that like Jesus, the youth will continually entrust themselves to You who judges righteously. Jesus, You bore the sins of the youth in Your body on the cross, so that the youth may die to sin and live to righteousness; for by Your wounds they were healed. Abba, even though they were straying like sheep, may they now return to You, the Shepherd and Guardian of their souls. Amen.

(1 Peter 2:19-25)

# PERSECUTION

Jesus, we thank You that when You suffered You were a good example of what it was like to be persecuted.  You were like a lamb led to the slaughter and did not even say a word.  Jesus, would You teach the youth to not say a word when they are being led like a lamb to the slaughter.  Would You show them when to speak and when to be silent as there is a time for both.  Lord, would You let them see Your glory like Stephen did when he was being stoned to death.  Jesus, You said we were called to suffer, so Lord we pray that You would prepare and protect the hearts of the youth for when persecution begins that they will know they are loved and  valued and that with You they can endure this.  In Jesus name we pray Amen!

(1 Peter 2:21, Acts 7:55-56, Romans 8:35-39)

# SUFFERING

Jesus, we pray that the youth would be ones who would not be afraid to suffer for Your name. Let them recognize that You suffered and You gave us an example that we would follow in Your steps. Teach them that if they are reviled not to revile in return, that when they suffer for Your name not to threaten, but instead to commit themselves to You who judges righteously. Thank You that You bore their sins in Your body on the tree that they should live to righteousness, for by Your stripes they are healed. Jesus, let them follow in Your example and walk in love, just like You did. Thank You for Your promise that the love that the Father has for You could be in us. Jesus, let these be the ones that You are looking for who will fulfill the mandate of God on their lives and be Your love on the earth to the lost. Thank You Jesus, amen.

(John 17:26, 1 Peter 2:21-24)

## OVERCOMER

Jesus, would You raise up this generation of
young people to be overcomers and a mighty
army in Canada!  Father, we press in for them
that they will not miss the call of God on their
lives, but will be the pure and spotless bride
calling with the Spirit, "Come Lord Jesus,
Come!"  Father, may they be the voice of one
crying in the wilderness, "Make straight the way
of the Lord!"  We prophesy to the four winds
and say breathe on these that they may live and
rise up a mighty army!

(Revelation 22:17, John 1:23, Ezra 37)

# UNITY

Father, we pray that the youth would be squeaky
clean pure. Jesus, we ask that You manifest
Your Name to them that the Father has given
You. These little ones are called to be Yours
and we pray that they would keep Your word.
May they come to know that everything that You
have has come from the Father and that they too
have access to it. We pray that they would
receive the words that You have given them. We
decree over the youth that they will understand
that Jesus has come from the Father. Jesus, we
know that You do not ask on behalf of the world,
but for those that the Father has called and given
You. Jesus, be glorified in them even though
You are no longer in the world, but because they
are still in the world. Holy Father, keep them in
Your name, the name You gave Jesus, so that
Your people would all be one as You and the
Father are One.

(John 17:6-11)

## LOVERS

Abba, we ask that You would fill the youth with
Your grace that teaches them to say no to
ungodliness and worldly passions, that they
might live soberly, righteously and godly in this
present age.  Raise them up as the light of the
world that cannot be hidden.  Fill them with
Your ferocious, unstoppable love that no matter
who opposes them, that they will not revile or
threaten in return, but instead that they will heap
coals of fire on their enemy.  Teach them to love
and bless their enemies.  Abba, raise them up far
above lukewarm religiosity that You hate, and
let them become the love of Christ which is the
true demonstration of knowing Christ.

(Titus 2:11-12, Proverbs 25:22, 1 Peter 2:21)

# SALVATION

Father, we ask that the Word of faith would be near the youth, in their mouths and in their hearts. Let them hear it over and over. Father, would You continue to place the gospel before them, so they have to make a decision about You. Place Your word in their hearts that even as they go about their activities, or are quiet, that Your Word would come to their minds and to their hearts! ABBA, may they be ones who will truly confess the Lord Jesus with their mouths and believe in their hearts that You raised Him from the dead, that they may truly and radically be saved! Father, may they be ones who will believe and become Your righteousness. May they see the fullness of what Jesus has done for them and truly believe You. Just as Abraham believed You and it was counted to him as righteousness, may the youth believe you and become the righteousness of God in Christ. Thank You that You are the Lord Our Righteousness. Jesus, may they confess You with their mouths that they may be saved. As repentance comes, we ask that they would have fruit worthy of repentance; that the confession of their mouth would result in action and a completely changed person! In Jesus' name!

(Romans 10:8-11, Romans 4:3, Jeremiah 23:6, Luke 3:8)

DAY 97

## ARISE

Abba, we call forth Your destiny over the youth,
in Jesus' name! We say, "Arise, shine; for your
light has come! And the glory of the LORD is
risen upon you. For behold, the darkness shall
cover the earth, and deep darkness the people;
but the LORD will arise over you, and His glory
will be seen upon you. The lost shall come to
your light, and kings to the brightness of your
rising."

(Isaiah 60:1-3)

# IMITATORS

Jesus, we declare over the youth, that they will be imitators of God as dear children. They will walk in love, as Christ also loves us and gave Himself for us, an offering and a sacrifice to God; a sweet-smelling aroma. We declare that they will walk as children of Light, for the fruit of the Spirit is in all goodness, righteousness and truth. They will find out what is acceptable to the LORD and will have no fellowship with the unfruitful works of darkness, but rather expose them. Daddy, we pray that the youth would be good Bereans; that they would hear the word, receive it with all readiness and search the scriptures daily to see if what they are hearing is true. Thank You for the seed that has been sown into their lives, Jesus, and we pray that it not be stolen from them, but let it be continually watered, so it can grow! Thank You that You are going after them, Jesus! Abba, let these be the ones!!!

(Ephesians 5:1-2, Ephesians 5:8-11, Acts 17:11)

# OVERCOMER

Abba, let the youth be fearless. Raise up an army of youth who will not go home because they are afraid even if they are given the chance, but will be the ones who pass the test to the end and defeat the enemy. Open their eyes to see the army that is with You, Lord, so they won't be afraid. Let them know that in You, the One who is in us is so much greater than the one who is in the world. Open their eyes God, to clearly see all deceptions of the Laodicean church that they would not come under any of them. Call them out of the teachings of Jezebel and Balaam. Raise up an army that will see things for what they truly are and call forth the plumbline of God that will be kept pure and holy for the coming of Jesus. Let them be the ones who live out the gospel and love of Jesus that all men may know that You are God and that they are Your disciples! Let them not grow weary in doing good, but teach them to pray and believe and not give up. Give them the faith of Abraham who believed Your word, Abba, against all hope and therefore received the promise. Thank You that the youth are overcomers. Thank You Jesus! Amen.

(Judges 7:3-7, 2 Kings 6:17, Jude 24-25, Philippians 1:9-11, Romans 4:18)

# FEAR OF THE LORD

Jesus, would You raise up the youth to stand up
and say yes to You no matter what the cost.
Father, may they be ones who will not bow to any
other god, no matter how great the pressure.
We ask that they would stand in boldness and
trust and conviction and say, "Even if we are
thrown into the fire, our God whom we serve is
able to deliver us. But if not, let it be known to
you, that we DO NOT SERVE YOUR GODS,
nor will we worship the golden image which you
have set up." Jesus, we're asking for a people of
strong conviction, who see right and wrong the
way You see it and will not bow for
ANYTHING. Father, may they be ones who will
go into the furnace unafraid, knowing that they
have done what gives You great honour and
glory! You said that we are called to suffer for
righteousness, so we're asking that You would
raise us up as a people who have learned to
rejoice and have great joy in suffering for Your
Kingdom! Be honoured and glorified O God!
We love You! Put a fear of You in our hearts
and in the hearts of the youth, so that they would
fear You more than any king and more than any
fiery furnace. In Jesus' name!

(Daniel 3:8-27, 1 Peter 2:20-21)

# TRUST

We declare that the youth will lift up their eyes to the mountains. Where does their help come from? Their help comes from the Lord, who made heaven and earth. God, You will not allow their foot to slip and You do not slumber. Lord, You are their keeper. Lord You are their shade on their right hand. The sun will not smite them by day, nor the moon by night. Lord, You will protect them from all evil; You will keep their soul. We thank You LORD, for guarding their going out and their coming in from this time forth and forever.

(Psalm 121)

# HOLINESS

Thank You Jesus for every youth that You have
made and have called to live a holy and
blameless life! Thank You that the law of the
Spirit of Life sets each one of the youth free
from the law of sin and death. The law was
powerless, so God, You sent Your own Son! We
know that the law is good if one uses it properly.
We also know that the law is made not for the
righteous, but for lawbreakers. Would You raise
up godly and pure, holy and righteous ones to
love and honour their parents. Help the youth to
live according to sound doctrine that conforms
to the gospel concerning the glory of the blessed
God, which You entrusted to each one of us!

(Romans 8:2-5, 1 Timothy 8-11)

## ENCOUNTER

Father, would You raise up the youth to be ones who will hear about You and then go and search You out for themselves. God, we ask that they would not wait for someone else to lead them to You, but would follow You themselves to find out Who You are, and what You are doing, and where You stay. Father, may they find You and then go out and tell their friends and siblings, "We found the Messiah!!" Jesus, may they hear and believe You with simple faith. Father, may they be like the shepherds who heard and immediately went and found out for themselves if what they had been told was true. May they see Jesus and then believe with all their hearts and go and proclaim what they have seen and heard.

(John 2:35-42, Luke 2:15-20)

# FIRE

Abba, encounter the youth with Your fire that so burns with life and passion in them that they cannot remain silent.  Fill them with Your fire, Abba, that is shut up in their bones that they cannot hold it.  Fill them with Your life- Your living water that will flow out of their belly as a river of living water!  Let them count everything as loss that they may gain Christ.  Fill them with Your life that never dies.  Let them burn with Your fire and life and passion that no matter who opposes them they will not quit, because they are filled with all the fullness of God.

(Jeremiah 20:9, Philippians 3:8-9, Ephesians 3:19)

## GRACE

Thank You Jesus for the youth.  Open their eyes to clearly be able to discern between good and evil, pure and defiled, what is yuck and what is pleasing to You.  Let the god of this world no longer be able to blind them, but Abba, we thank You that You are giving them sight.  Give them great wisdom, truth and discernment, and also the grace to act on it.  Lord, cause them to walk out of movie theaters, or sketchy parties and be powerful voices for righteousness in their homes, schools, towns and shopping centers.  Raise up a great company of youth who will not be able to remain silent about the truth, but will be compelled by love to speak in Jesus' name. Abba, let them truly see the light of the glory of the gospel displayed in the face of Christ who is the image of God.  Let them no longer call evil good and good evil, in Jesus' name.

(2 Corinthians 4:4, Titus 2:12, Isaiah 5:20)

# DEVOTED

Jesus, we ask that the youth would make a decision to follow You once and for all. Father, would You bring them to a place of decision, where they have to choose whom they will serve, and may their cry be, "As for me and my house, we will serve the Lord!" Jesus, we ask that they would cry out for You, the Fountain of Living Water, and the Bread of Life, and eat of You, that they would never thirst again, but that Your water would be springing up in them to everlasting life. Father, let them see You. Open their eyes to the truth of who You are, that when You say, "I AM" that they would believe You and be radically transformed by You. Jesus, we ask that, like it was for You, their food would be to do the Father's will and to finish His work. May they cry out, "Now we believe, not because of what anyone said, for we ourselves have heard Him and we know that this is indeed the Christ, the Savior of the world!" Abba, may they be wholly given to You!

(Joshua 24:15, John 4:14, John 4:25-42)

## DISCIPLESHIP

Father, we pray that the heart of each youth would declare, "But I, Your servant, have feared Jehovah from my youth." Do not remember the sins of their youth, or their rebellions; according to Your mercy remember them for Your goodness' sake, O Jehovah. O God, teach them from their youth and we cry out that the youth would declare Your wonderful works. Remember now, youth, your Creator in the days of your youth. We prophesy over the youth, "Cry out to God, our Father, 'You are the guide of my youth.'"

(Psalm 71:17, 1 Kings 18:12, Psalm 25:7, Ecclesiastes 12:1, Jeremiah 3:4)

# BELIEVE

Father, we ask that the youth would believe in
Jesus and never look back. Father, would You
draw them and place such a hunger inside of
them to search You out that they will truly find
who You are and believe in You! May there be a
cry in their heart, "Even if everyone else falls
away, Lord, to whom shall we go? You have the
words of eternal life." May they be ones who
come to believe and know that You are the
Christ, the Son of the Living God and give
themselves completely to You! Father, we ask
that no matter who comes and goes, that You
would ground these youth in You that they
would put their hand to the plow and never look
back, but follow after You; that come what may,
despite persecution, they would overcome; they
would walk with You in white, for they would be
found worthy.

(John 6:68, John 6:69, Luke 9:62, Revelation 3:4)

## LOVE

Jesus, thank You for Your incredible love for the youth. Thank You that Your love for them knows no limits. Abba, we ask that You would reveal to each of the youth individually the power of Your love that there is nothing that can separate them from Your love. Not death, nor life, nor angels, nor principalities, nor powers, nor things present, nor things to come, nor height, nor depth, nor any other creature shall be able to separate them from the love of God, which is in Christ Jesus our Lord. Let them be fully convinced of Your love in their own minds, that they will live out of the fullness of that truth.

(Romans 8:38-39)

# ENDURANCE

Abba, we thank You for the youth who will run
the race with endurance, that they will not look
to the right nor the left; they will be ones to run
after You! Jesus, let this generation run to You
and be obedient to Your heart! Let it not take a
storm, or a fish to swallow them before they
repent and obey. Holy Spirit, would You reveal
the nature of God to the youth and help them to
see the truth.

(Hebrews 12:1-3, Jonah 1, 1 Corinthians 2:10)

# EYES TO SEE

May we hear of the faith of the youth in the Lord
Jesus and their love to all the saints. We will not
cease giving thanks for them, making mention of
them in our prayer time, that You God, the God
of our Lord Jesus Christ, the Father of glory,
may give them the Spirit of Wisdom and
Revelation in the knowledge of You. That the
eyes of their understanding being enlightened,
they may know what is the hope of Your calling
God, and what is the riches of the glory of Your
inheritance in the saints. The surpassing
greatness of Your power toward them, the ones
believing, according to the working of Your
mighty strength which You worked in Christ in
raising Him from the dead. You, Father, seated
Him at Your right hand in the heavenlies, far
above all principality and authority and power
and dominion and every name being named, not
only in this world, but also in the coming age.
And You Father have put all things under Jesus'
feet and gave Him to be Head over all things to
the church, which is His body, the fullness of
Him who fills all in all. May the Youth receive
You and partake of Your Spirit. Fill them with
grace, O God, and compel them with Your
love!

(Ephesians 1:15-23)

# INTIMACY

Abba, let the youth be like Enoch who walked
with You and let them intimately know You.
Thank You God that You have shown them
what is good and what You require of them; to
do justice, to love mercy and to walk humbly with
their God.

(Genesis 5:22-24, Micah 6:8)

## PURITY

Jesus, would You raise up the youth in purity
and holiness, who will be unashamed to walk in
complete holiness before You, completely
undefiled. Daddy, would You teach them to see
the distinction between righteousness and
wickedness, and choose what is true and right,
and pure and lovely, and holy and blameless.
May they love You more than anything else or
any opinion of others. Father, we ask that in
everything, they would seek to honour You
above anyone else. In Jesus' name.

(John 5:44)

# BELIEVE

Jesus, we thank You for the youth and who You
are calling them to be! Thank You God that
You called forth things that are not yet so as
though they were, and that if we believe You for
it, it will be credited to us as righteousness! Lord
Jesus, we ask that You would rise up the youth
to be whole hearted lovers of You, Jesus, and
that they would leave nothing behind. Open
their eyes to the hypocrisy, so that they can be
whole-hearted lovers of You, Jesus. Teach the
youth to guard their heart for it is the wellspring
of life. Keep them on the narrow path; let them
be some of the few that find it. Let them find
You as they seek for You with their whole
heart. Open their hearts to hear the message of
the gospel and BELIEVE in the simplicity of the
cross. In Your name we pray. Amen!

(Romans 4:3, Proverbs 4:23)

## UNITY

LORD, we pray that the youth would continue
to have unity in the same way that You do. You
Father, are in Jesus and Jesus is in You. We
pray that they may be united with You, so that
the world may know and believe that You have
sent Jesus into the world. In this way, the area
they reside in will know that the Father has sent
the Son and that You love them the same way
that You have loved Jesus.

(John 17:20-23)

# OVERCOMER

Father, we ask that the youth would not despise
Your patience, but that Your goodness would
lead them to repentance. Father, we ask that
Your kingdom would come upon them. May
they know You, Lord Jesus, and be ones who
will, by patiently continuing in doing good, seek
for glory and honour and immortality, so that
they may obtain eternal life. Jesus, we ask that
they would be doers of Your word and not
merely hearers. We decree that these youth are
overcomers who will be dressed in white, whose
names will not be blotted out of the Lamb's
Book of Life, but that Jesus will be able to
confess their names before the Father. Draw
them O God!

(Romans 2:4-13, Revelation 3:5)

## CRY

LORD, we pray that the youth will cry out to You, and when they do, that You, O God, will give heed to their prayers. May they call to You from the ends of the earth if their hearts grow faint. Lead them to the Rock, for You are their place of refuge, a tower of strength against the enemy. May they dwell in Your tent forever. Let them take refuge in the shelter of Your wings.

(Psalm 61:1-4)

# PURITY

Jesus, have Your way amongst the youth.  Create in them a pure heart, O God, and renew a steadfast spirit within them, so that they may dwell in the house of the Lord forever!  May they be one as You and the Father are one.  Make them pure, so that they may dwell with You forever and ever, amen!

(Psalm 51:10, John 17:22-23)

## GOSPEL

Jesus, thank You for the Youth. Jesus, we ask that You would open their eyes to see that You have made a way for them to be adopted by the King and that You would be their Abba Father. Let them see the gospel for what it really is; may they know that who You set free is free indeed. The youth no longer have to go on sinning, but through Your Spirit, they can put to death the deeds of the body, so they will live. Thank You Jesus that You gave Yourself for the youth to redeem them from all iniquity and to purify for Yourself Your own special people zealous for good works.

(John 8:36, Romans 8:11-14, Titus 2:14)

# TRUTH

Thank You Jesus, that You Yourself bore our sins in Your body on the tree, that being dead to sin, this generation should live to righteousness, by Your stripes we have been healed.  Abba, let the youth know and understand this truth and live out the fullness of Your gospel.

(1Peter 2:24)

# HOLINESS

Father, thank You for the calling that You have on these youth to be in You! Jesus, You said that You are light and there is no darkness in You at all, so we ask that You would raise them up to believe You that it is possible to be in You and have no darkness in them either. We decree that they are a people who will not compromise and make excuses for darkness when there are none in the Bible. We decree that this is a people of radical faith who will believe what You say and live it out. We decree that this is a people of purity and holiness who will walk in the fullness of God and not sin. Father, thank You that it is by grace that we have been saved through faith, and it's not from us, it's a gift of God. We're asking for that gift of grace to come upon the youth right now, that Your truth, Your desire, Your heart and Your righteousness would so be revealed to them that they would hate anything that dishonours You and glorifies darkness. We decree that they are ones who will love the light and come to the Light because they obey You. We decree that this is a generation who will so walk in the Spirit, that they will not fulfill the lusts of the flesh.

(Galatians 5:16, John 3:19-21, 1 John 1:5, Ephesians 2:8-9)

# FOUNDATION

Abba, let the youth be fully persuaded that
neither tribulation, nor distress, nor persecution,
nor famine, nor nakedness, nor peril nor sword,
nor death, nor life, nor principalities, nor
powers, nor things present, nor things to come,
nor height, nor depth, nor any other creature can
separate them from the love of God in Christ
Jesus our Lord.  Abba, raise up the youth who
will know Your word and not just be hearers, but
doers of the word; that their lives will be firmly
grounded on Your truth, that their foundation
will not be sinking sand.

(Romans 8:35-39, Matthew 7:24-27, James 1:22-25)

## TRUTH

Father, we pray that the youth would prosper in
every way and be in good health physically and
spiritually.  LORD, we are so excited to see that
You are moving on them and pray that You will
continue to pursue them with Your love.  Father,
we know that You have no greater joy than to
hear that Your children are living according to
the TRUTH!  We pray that the youth would be
faithful in all things and that their love would be
a testimony right across the nation!

(3 John 1:1-6)

# GRACE

Thank You for the youth and who You are rising
them up to be; mighty warriors for the Kingdom
of God! Raise them up to be ones that will be
like the Davids, who will fight the Goliaths of
abortion; like Gideons who will tear down the
idols in their father's house; and like the Esthers,
who stand up for such a time as this. Jesus,
thank You for giving them the character needed
to see Your Kingdom come here on earth as it is
in heaven! Jesus, we pray for the Titus 2 grace-
the grace of God that has appeared, bringing
salvation for all people, training us to renounce
ungodliness and worldly passions, and to live
self-controlled, upright, and godly lives in the
present age. Help the youth to wait for You, our
blessed hope, looking for the hope of the
appearing of the glory of our great God and
Savior Jesus Christ. You gave Yourself for the
youth to redeem them from all lawlessness and
to purify them for Yourself a people for Your
own possession who are zealous for good
works.

(Titus 2:13-14)

# OBEDIENCE

DAY 126

Father, we ask that it would be said of the youth that the ruler of this world has nothing in them, just like he had nothing in Jesus. Father, we ask that they would be ones who have Jesus' commandments and keep them- truly loving Jesus! Jesus, may they be ones who love You, because they are loved by the Father, and You Jesus, will love them and manifest Yourself to them. May they truly love You Jesus! You promised that those who love You and keep Your word, the Father would love and You would come and make Your home with them. Jesus, we are asking that this generation would love You so well that You can make Your home with them. Father, we're asking for the holiness to come, so that You can abide with them, not just visit once, but manifest Yourself and stay. We love You Jesus and You are worth it all to us, so we pray that You would raise up a people who would value You and Your presence enough to get rid of anything that hinders. Lord, that they would make themselves available to host Your presence and Your glory. You can do it Jesus! May they be ones who are in You so fully that the enemy has NOTHING in them. In Jesus' name.

(John 14:21-23, John 14:30)

# PURITY

LORD, please give the youth a hunger for Your word and that they would long for every fact to be established according to Your word. LORD, give them the courage to examine themselves according to Your word to see if they are actually in the faith; if they indeed pass Your test. Father, empower the youth to live for the truth, so that it would be impossible for them to live according to anything contrary. We pray that the youth would become fully mature even at young ages. May they continually rejoice in Your presence and be filled with Your peace.

(2 Corinthians 13:5)

## OUTPOURING

Thank You Jesus so much for the youth that
You are raising up to be leaders in this
generation. Thank You that You promise to
pour out Your Spirit on all flesh, that Your sons
and daughters will prophesy. Jesus, we remind
You of Your promises and we thank You that
Your word will never return to You void, but it
will accomplish what You please and it will
prosper in the thing for which You sent it. God
would You do it now. Pour out Your Spirit on
the youth, that they would know You. That they
would know the power of Your love and the
power of the Gospel. We pray the youth would
long to know nothing, but Christ and Him
crucified, and that they would boast about
nothing but the cross. Thank You Jesus.

(Joel 2:28, Isaiah 55:11, 1 Corinthians 2:2,
Galatians 6:14)

# LOVE

Jesus, You are amazing and we thank You for
the children You have blessed us with to pray
for. Jesus, we pray that You would rise up
children after Your own heart who will
encourage and bless one another. May they be a
generation who would so love You and love each
other as they love themselves. Jesus, may they
be the most honouring, giving and thankful
generation known to man! Holy Spirit, would
You show them how to pray continually and give
thanks in everything! May they be good
stewards of what they have been blessed with!!!
Jesus, thank You for these youth. Thank You
that You have blessed them with every spiritual
blessing.

(1 Thessalonians 5:14-16, Ephesians 1:3, Luke 10:27)

DAY 129

## ADOPTION

Thank you Jesus that You have blessed the youth. You predestined them for adoption, before the foundations of the earth. You thought about them. You called them your very own, Hephzibah- My delight is in her- a city not forsaken. Jesus, we pray that they would be firmly established in Your love, abounding more and more in it. Let faith and hope arise, in Jesus name amen!

(Ephesians 1:3-5, Isaiah 62:4)

# EVANGELISM

LORD, fill the youth with a passion and desire to enter into their homes and schools, speaking in such a way that that a great number of both family and classmates would believe. Protect them against those who would refuse to believe their message about You, so that the unbelieving will not stir up or poison the minds of those who have not yet decided.

(Acts 14:1-2)

# HUNGER

Abba, let the youth be captivated by nothing but
You and Your magnificence and glory.
Captivate their affection, their gaze and their
dreams. Thank You that Your thoughts toward
them are more than the sands of the sea. Would
You be their One thing, Jesus; that the one thing
that they ask and seek would be to dwell in Your
house and to behold Your beauty and inquire in
Your temple. Thank You Jesus. Fill them with
a hunger and thirsting for righteousness, that
they might be satisfied with You Jesus; in Your
presence. Let them know that one day in Your
courts is better than a thousand elsewhere.

(Psalm 139:18, Matthew 5:6, Psalm 84:10)

## OBEDIENCE

Father, we ask that You would raise up the youth in this area to be ones who truly love You, who keep Your commandments and it's not a burden to them. May they be ones who are born of You, who believe that Jesus is Your Son, and have great faith, so that they will overcome the world. We're asking that they would not be afraid to believe You for the big things, but that they would trust that all You say is true and available to them if they will grab hold of You. In Jesus' name!!!

(1 John 5:3)

# GOD CHASERS

Father, we ask that the Youth would be ones
who respond to You like the shepherds did.
Father, may they hear Your voice, hear Your
message, Your gospel, Your decree; the good
news of great joy that Jesus has truly saved us
and set us free, and BELIEVE YOU! Jesus, we
ask that they will be so radically impacted by
You, and will so radically believe You that they
will run and hurry to find out if what You said
was true! ABBA, we're asking that as they've
heard about You that they would run to find
You and search You out, no matter what the
cost. We pray that they would not even wait for
a more convenient time, but that they would
leave everything they're doing and run after
You! Jesus, You promised that if they would
seek You with all of their hearts, they would find
You. Abba, may they find You and return with
great joy, telling everyone around them of Who
You are and what You have done!!! Jesus, may
they be so undone by You, that their automatic
response is to give You great glory and praise for
all that You have done!!! In Jesus' name!!!

(Luke 2:10-20)

# ENDURANCE

Abba, thank You that You are calling the youth into Your radical love that covers over a multitude offenses.  Your love that casts out all fear, Your love that sets them free.  Where the Spirit of the Lord is there is freedom.  We declare freedom over the youth, in Jesus' name. Abba, we ask that You would radically encounter the youth in such a real way that there is no denying that You are their Savior, and that You are alive, and that You are their Lord. Jesus, let the youth be ready when the end times come that they would not be the ones who are deceived, that they will not be offended no matter how much they are afflicted or hurt. Jesus, let their love not grow cold, but let them be the ones who will endure to the end and be saved.  Jesus, let them be the ones who are watching, waiting and ready for You.

(Matthew 24:4-13, Matthew 24:42-46)

## DRAWING

Jesus, we thank You that You are rising up a youth who will not be offended because of the gospel that is being preached!  Thank You that they will seek Your Kingdom first and they would be honoured above all peoples for searching the scriptures!  Jesus, would You draw each youth to Your heart.  Reveal the Father, Abba; reveal Your Son to this generation, so they can do the greater works that You promised us.

(Matthew 6:33, Matthew 11:6, Acts 17:11, John 6:44, John 14:12)

# SEEK

Thank You Jesus for the youth and that You
created them to seek You with their whole
heart. Would You give them the spirit of
wisdom and revelation that they may know You
better. We pray that each one of the youth
would thirst for the water that never runs dry;
the living water which those who drink from will
never thirst again. Let Your Kingdom come and
Your will be done here on earth as it is in
heaven.

(Ephesians 1:17, John 4:7-15, Luke 11:2-4a)

DAY 137

## OVERCOMERS

We declare that this is a generation born of God, who will overcome the world!!!  This is the victory that overcomes the world, FAITH!!!  We declare that these are youth who overcome the world, ones who believe that Jesus is the Son of God!!!  We declare that this is a generation who will LOVE GOD; ones who keep His commandments, and Your commands  are not a burden to them!

(1 John 5:4-5)

# BLESSED

O LORD our God, raise up a generation of Annas who seek You night and day in prayer and fasting. Father, we cry out for great grace for the youth to fast and pray. We cry out for a generation that would seek after You; a generation desiring You, Your kingdom and Your righteousness. We seek a generation longing for Your Spirit as a bride longs for her bridegroom. LORD, we pray for a great hunger and thirst in the youth! We declare over the youth, "Blessed are the youth who are poor in spirit! For theirs is the kingdom of Heaven. Blessed are the youth that mourn, for they shall be comforted! Blessed are the youth who are meek for they shall inherit the earth! Blessed are the youth who hunger and thirst after righteousness for they shall be filled! Blessed are the youth who are merciful for they shall obtain mercy! Blessed are the youth who are pure in heart for they shall see God! Blessed are the youth who are peacemakers for they shall be called the sons of God! Blessed are the youth who have been persecuted for righteousness sake for theirs is the kingdom of Heaven! Blessed are the youth when men revile them and persecute them, because they say all kinds of evil against the youth falsely, for Jesus' sake. Rejoice YOUTH and be exceedingly glad, for your reward in Heaven is great. For so they persecuted the prophets who were before you!"

(Matthew 5:3-12, Luke 2:36-37, Matthew 6:33, Revelation 21:2)

DAY 139

## LEADERSHIP

Jesus, we pray that You will protect the youth. May they see Your glory. Just as Moses wouldn't go into the promised land without You, would You build such a tenacity in them that they would not leave without You; that they would they cry out for You to go with them. Rise up tenacious leaders who will lead well and seek Your heart and do the greater works! Lead them in Your ways, that they may find favour with You. May this be a generation You are well pleased with.

(Exodus 33:13-18)

# FRUIT

Jesus, thank You for the youth. Let them be
ones who will steward well what You have
entrusted to them. Thank You that You have
given them many different gifts. Let them be
faithful in the little, so that You can entrust them
with much. Let them no longer be slaves, but
friends of God, to whom You tell all the things
of God. Thank You Jesus, that they will not only
bear a little bit of fruit or bring a little increase
for Your kingdom, but they will be the ones who
bear much fruit to the glory of Your name. Let
them use the five talents to bring ten and lay
them all at Your feet to the glory of Your
name. We ask that they would even see Your
love and truth in its fullness. Thank You Jesus
for Your sacrifice and Your gift of love for all of
humanity. Give them great grace to celebrate
You today and not the celebration of the world.
Let the youth abide in You, that they will bear
much fruit. Thank You Jesus for Your love.
Amen.

(Matthew 25:14-30, John 15:15, John 15:8, John 15:15,
Romans 2:6, 1 Corinthians 12:4)

# ZEAL

LORD, Your heart's desire and prayer is concerning the salvation of the youth. Father, they are pulled in so many different directions. There is a way that seems right to them, but in the end it only leads to death; spiritually and for some, physically. Father, we pray that a testimony begins about them, that they would have a zeal for You filled with knowledge of You. We pray that the youth would know that there is no high like the Most High and that there is no substance that can bring joy and fulfillment like being filled with the Holy Spirit. Father, we pray that the youth would have a zeal based on knowledge of Your word and not just running on emotion or experience. Holy Spirit, we ask that You help them to be established in Your righteousness and not a righteousness established outside of You. We ask that You fill them with a submissive spirit that would yield itself to the Holy Spirit.

(Romans 10:1-3, Proverbs 14:12)

# LOVERS

Jesus, we thank You that You are willing to rise up young rulers that will love you with everything they have; that they would be willing to sell all they have and be sold out for the gospel. Would You stir in them a godly jealousy that would cause the Youth to pursue You more. Thank You that Your arm is not too short to save! Jesus, we thank You that greater works will be done here on earth as it is in heaven! In Your name, we thank You and praise You! Amen.

(2 Kings 22, Mark 10:17-31, Isaiah 59:1,
2 Corinthians 2:11, Hebrews 10:24)

# FAITH

Father, we thank You that You love giving good gifts. We pray that You would endow the youth with the gift of faith, so that they could be assured of what they are hoping for and be certain of what they do not see. Abba, we know that it is by faith that they will understand that the world was prepared by Your word, so that what is seen was not made out of things that are visible. It is wild and amazing that You are able to do that. The youth are continually indoctrinated by falsehood and need great faith to be able to overcome these obstacles. LORD, we are asking for a kind of faith that would invoke a simple obedience, honour and a trust that would change the course of history. You said that we had the ability to quicken the time and we are asking that You would place that on the hearts of the youth in this region. We ask these things so that Your name would be glorified and made famous in this generation.

(2 Peter 3:12, Hebrews 11:1-3)

## FOLLOWER

Jesus, thank You that You have the words of eternal life. We ask, Abba, that You would put Your resolve in the youth to follow You wherever You go and let them be ones who say, "Where else should we go? You have the words of eternal life." No matter what You call other people to, let the youth pick up their cross and follow You. God, let them be ones who will loudly and clearly cry out, "Yes, Lord! Send me, I will go."

(John 6:68, Matthew 16:24, Isaiah 6:8)

## ENCOUNTER

Thank You Jesus for Your word and it is good!!! Abba, thank You for Your Son and that we can run after Him. Abba, we pray that You would instill such boldness and tenacity and love for You that the youth would be willing to leave house and home, mother and father and lay it all down for the sake of Your Kingdom, knowing there are rewards that await those who obey! Holy Spirit, would You encounter each youth in such a personal way that they would know without a doubt they have encountered YOU, the Living God! Holy Spirit, You are the Comforter and You will comfort all those who are mourning; in every trial and tribulation You are there, and are pouring out Your love from the Father. Thank You and we bless Your name! Amen!

(Matthew 29:19, Matthew 5:4, Acts 2, Romans 5:3-5)

# FIND

Father, we ask that You would instruct the youth
even in the night watch. You are the Lord who
has given counsel, so we ask that the youth
would hear You and obey. Jesus, may they be
ones who set You always before themselves and
ones who are unmovable because You are at
their right hand. Father, may they have great joy
in following after You and being Yours! May
they follow Your path of life for them and find
the narrow gate that leads to life. Jesus, we ask
that they could find You! Would You draw
them O God! God, would You show them the
path of life. We pray that the Youth would be
ones who find fullness of joy in Your presence,
and their greatest pleasures, forever, at Your
right hand. Thank You that You open Your
hand and satisfy the desire of every living thing,
so we ask that You would teach them to look to
You first for everything.

(Psalm 16:7-11, Psalm 145:16)

## LOVE

Father, we ask that You raise up the youth to be
passionately in love with You.  Would You teach
us how to love them well.  Abba, we ask that we
would be ones who would very gladly spend and
be spent for their souls.  Show us how to pray, O
God!  Show us how to fight for those who are
lost and lonely and dying and searching for
You!  Daddy, would You do for them what You
have done for us?  Cause them to know the love
that You have for them.  Daddy, would You
raise us up as a mighty army all running together
for Your Kingdom and Your glory!

(2 Corinthians 12:14-15)

# PEACE

Daddy, right now we ask that You would comfort any of the youth that are hurting and mourning. Fill them with Your peace that passes all understanding. That's not just a cliché or overused scripture that has no effect, that's Your promises that Your peace that passes all understanding WILL guard their hearts and minds in Christ Jesus as they make their requests known to You. Teach them to be anxious for nothing, but in everything by prayer and supplication with thanksgiving, to let their requests be made known to You in Jesus' name. Teach them to pray without ceasing and to give thanks in everything for this is the will of God in Christ Jesus concerning them. Let them not quench the Spirit and not despise prophesying, but teach them to test all things and to hold fast to what is good. Teach them to abstain from all appearance of evil. Let the very God of peace sanctify the youth completely, and we pray that their whole spirit and soul and body would be preserved blameless to the coming of our Lord Jesus Christ. You are faithful, Jesus, and You will also do it. Let them be ones who will not pay back evil for evil, but follow after what is good, both among themselves and to all men. Encounter each one of them, Daddy. Draw them to Your heart in Jesus' name. Thank You that You love each of them with the same love that You love Jesus.

(Philippians 4:6-7, 1 Thessalonians 5:15-24, John 17:23)

## HONOUR

Father, we pray that the youth will develop a
love and honour for those in leadership, that
they would follow the rules and ordinances even
from those with whom they may not agree with,
so long as they are not asking them to sin,
knowing that this is well pleasing to You.
Father, help them to discern the difference
between submitting to those in authority over
them and needing to say no to ungodliness and
worldly passions.  Holy Spirit, may You be what
woos them and that religion will be a sour taste
in their mouths that they would spit out.  May
they press for the truth and for Your presence
with an insatiable hunger for Your word.

(Matthew 23:3, Exodus 20:12)

## ZEAL

Jesus, we pray that you would raise up the youth,
that they would not be lacking in diligence, but
they would serve You enthusiastically! Raise up
your zealous warriors for the kingdom of God
who would have the knowledge and passion that
would be sustained with Your GREAT
LOVE!!!

(Romans 12:11, Romans 10:13)

# TRUTH

Holy Spirit, thank You for coming to counsel the
world. Thank You for loving us enough to
convict us about sin, righteousness and
judgment. You convict us of sin because people
have not believed in You, of righteousness
because Jesus has gone to be with the Father,
and about judgment because the ruler of this
world has been judged- praise God! Holy Spirit,
You are the Spirit of Truth and we pray that You
will fill the youth with Your truth because You
do not speak of Your own accord, but You speak
whatever You hear from God. We pray that the
youth will have ears to hear You as You declare
to them what is to come.

(John 16:7-13)

# IDENTITY

Jesus, we ask that our sons may be as plants grown up in their youth.  Let our daughters be as cornerstones who are cut for the structure of a palace.  Let our granaries be full, providing all kinds of produce.  May our sheep bring forth thousands in our fields.  May our cattle be heavy with young, suffering no mishap or failure in bearing; that there would be no cry of distress in our streets, because blessed are the people of whom this is true.  Blessed are the people whose God is the Lord.  Let that be true of the youth in our country.  Raise up the young people who, although they may be uneducated, everyone will be able to see by their courage that they have been with Jesus.  Raise up youth who are not like the culture has defined youth, but who will be mature leaders in their region like Timothy was, and who are polished in righteousness and holiness as the temple of the Holy Spirit.  Thank You Jesus.  No longer are young people going to be defined by what culture names them, but by the truth that God says about them.  They are a chosen generation, a royal priesthood, Your own special people called to show forth the praises of You who called them out of darkness into Your marvelous light!  Amen and amen!

(Psalm 144:12-15, Acts 4:13)

# WHOLENESS

Jesus, thank You that every storm, every sickness, every demon has to obey You.  Father, we pray that You would put a knowing and a desire in the hearts of the youth that if they can only touch Jesus, they will be made whole.  LORD, we ask that You would put such a burning hunger in them to touch You that they will pursue after You and touch You even if other people are watching, even if it's inconvenient timing.  Father, may they be relentless in their pursuit of You.  Jesus, we ask that they would turn to You with their brokenness and addictions and find healing in You.  We decree wholeness over them from this very hour.  We ask that You would stir great faith in them to believe You for healing.  We decree hope and wholeness over this generation in Jesus' name!

(Matthew 9:20-22)

# FOLLOWERS

We proclaim the blessing of God over the youth. May the LORD enable each of the youth to find security in the house of God. Father, we pray that You will send forth fathers and mothers in the faith that would love each of the youth well; men and women of integrity who would cause them to follow You wherever You go, wherever You would have them live and go to school and work. We pray that the youth would be Your people and You would be their God. We proclaim and decree the determination of God over the youth that will not be persuaded to turn to the right or left, but that Jesus would be their focal point. God, conquer their hearts and make them new. Father, mold and form them into Your image and show them the adventure and ecstasy of loving You!

(Ruth 1:9, Ruth 1:16, Ruth 1:18)

# KINGDOM MINDED

Father, You said that the end of all things is at hand; therefore, be serious and watchful in your prayers. Father, we pray that You would teach the youth along with us how to do that. Even as we continue praying for the youth in our area, would You help us to watch and pray, to pray on the mark, fervently; prayers that are powerful and effective. Thank You that You are once more shaking not only the earth, but heaven also, so that everything that can be shaken is removed, and only what cannot be shaken remains. Father, we pray that the youth would go after what cannot be shaken. Would You give them a desire to go after You and Your Kingdom. We declare that things of the world will no longer have an attraction for them, but that they will be ones who receive a kingdom which cannot be shaken. Father, we ask that they would have eyes to see the difference between righteousness and wickedness; what is temporal, and what remains. Father, give them a complete dissatisfaction with everything of the world, so that they would long for You and pursue after You as the One who remains! We ask that You would give them grace to serve You acceptably with reverence and godly fear, knowing that You are a consuming fire. Father, may they not refuse You, who speaks from Heaven.

(1 Peter 4:7, James 5:16, Hebrews 12:25-28, Malachi 3:18)

# GOOD FRUIT

Jesus, thank You for the youth and for their radical boldness. Help them use it for Your glory Jesus! Help each youth to delight in Your law; that they would be ones to meditate on it day and night! May they be like trees planted by the streams of water that yield fruit in their season- fruit that will not whither. May they bear much fruit- fruit that will last! Jesus we are asking for true salvation. Let it be real. Let them not be deceived- whoever does what it right is righteous and whoever does not is of the devil, so God may it be kept real in Jesus!

(Psalm 1, John 15:5-9, 1 John 3:10)

DAY 157

# WISDOM

Jesus, we ask that You would grow the fear of the Lord in the youth. The fear of the Lord which is to hate evil, pride and arrogance. The fear of the Lord that is the beginning of wisdom and that is a fountain of life, to depart from the snares of death. Jesus, let them incline their ear to wisdom and apply their hearts to understanding. Let them cry after knowledge and lift up their voice for understanding. Let them seek her as silver and search for her as for hidden treasures, so that they shall understand the fear of the Lord and find the knowledge of God. Let wisdom enter their hearts and knowledge be pleasant to their souls; to deliver them from the way of the evil one, from the men of perverted speech, who leave the path of uprightness to walk in the ways of darkness, from those who deliver them to the forbidden woman and the adulteress who flatters with her words, who forsakes the companion of her youth and forgets the covenant of her God. Father, would you cause sexual immorality to sink down to death and for the fear of the Lord to remain, so the youth will walk in the way of the good and keep to the paths of the righteous. Thank You Jesus.

(Proverbs 8:13, Proverbs 9:10, Proverbs 14:26-27, Proverbs 2)

# RIGHTEOUSNESS

Father, we pray that the youth will seek first Your kingdom and Your righteousness.  For the kingdom of God is not a matter of eating and drinking, but of righteousness, peace and joy in the Holy Spirit; whoever serves Christ in this way is pleasing to You, God, and approved by men.  Lord, we pray that the youth would experience the fullness of Your joy in all of the fullness of the Holy Spirit as they drink of Your Spirit!  We pray for Your peace that surpasses all understanding to encompass them.  And Father we ask that You would create circumstances in their lives that would grow Your righteousness in them.

(Matthew 6:33, Romans 14:17-18, Philippians 4:7, Ephesians 5:18)

# REFUGE

Jesus, thank You for the youth.  Abba, would You let them taste and see Your goodness that they cannot deny that You are real and that You are good.  Let them take refuge in You, Jesus.  Would You be their refuge and strength, a very present help in trouble.  Right now we ask, Jesus, that if any of the youth are in trouble and don't know where to turn, that You would fix their eyes on You.  Let them turn to You that the veil would be removed from their eyes, that they could see You and know that Your goodness is so much better than they ever knew.  Even when they don't know what to do, let them be like Jehoshaphat who didn't know what to do, but his eyes were on You.  Thank You Jesus that they will no longer turn to the things of this world to fill the emptiness, but they will seek You with all their heart and find You Jesus.

(Psalm 24:8, Psalm 46:1, 2 Corinthians 3:16,
2 Chronicles 20:12, Jeremiah 29:13)

# REVELATION

Jesus, thank You that You are the Truth, the
Way, and the Life.  No one can come to the
Father except through You!  Your Word is
pretty clear, Abba, that NO ONE can come to
You unless they come through Jesus.  All things
have been entrusted to You Jesus by Your
Father.  No one knows who You are except the
Father, and no one knows who the Father is
except You, so Jesus we are asking that You
would reveal the Father, and that His nature
would be made known at a quickened rate as
there is not much time.  LORD, remind us how
brief our time is on earth, that the days are
numbered.  How fleeting is life!  You have made
our life no longer than the width of our hand!
One's entire lifetime is just a moment to You; at
best, each of us is but a breath.  Teach the youth
how to number their days, so that they may grow
in wisdom and in the knowledge of Your love, so
that they may know the hope in which You
called them!  The Spirit and the bride say,
"Come!"

(John 14:6, John 3:35, Psalm 39:4-5, Psalm 90:12,
Ephesians 1:17-18, Revelation 22:17)

# INTEGRITY

Abba, we call out for youth without blemish, of good appearance and skillful in all wisdom, endowed with knowledge, competent to stand in the king's palace and able to learn the literature and language of the Kingdom. Jesus, let them sing of Your steadfast love and justice; to You Lord, let them make music. Let them ponder the way that is blameless. Teach them to walk with integrity of heart within their homes. Jesus, let them not set before their eyes anything that is worthless. Let them hate the work of those who fall away; it shall not cling to them. Let a perverse heart be far from them; that they will know nothing evil. Let them be truthful and humble in Jesus' name. Thank You that You look with favor on the faithful in the land that they may dwell with You. Let them walk in the way that is blameless that they shall minister to You, Abba. Let them practice honesty and be ones who are trusted with much. In Jesus' name.

(Daniel 1:4, Psalm 101)

# LIFE

Father, so many are still sitting at the tomb of
Jesus. They have brought spices and are
mourning because they cannot see You now or
fully hear You now. They are looking for Your
body, but cannot find it. Others are completely
perplexed because they thought they would find
You in places that are void of life. But God, we
thank You that You are sending messengers to
those who are searching for You to say, "Why
are you looking for the living among the dead?"
JESUS, You are alive! Jesus, may the youth find
You and find Your body among the living!

(Luke 24:1-5)

# THANKSGIVING

Thank You Jesus that the youth will overcome by the blood of the Lamb and the word of their testimony, and they will not love their own lives even when faced with death. Jesus, we thank You that they will love God and that money will have no hold on them. Thank You that they are a generation that will be humble, meek, modest, kind, obedient to parents, grateful, HOLY, loving, and forgiving. Thank You that the youth will encourage one another, be self-controlled, gentle, compassionate, and tender. They will love good and be LOYAL. Would You rise up the watchman who will be watchful and on guard; in humility they will count others more significant than themselves. Pleasure will not keep the Youth from obtaining salvation. They will be patient lovers of God!

(2 Timothy 3:2-4, Philippians 2:3, 1 Thessalonians 5:11, Revelation 12:11)

# THE CROSS

Abba, we ask that You would raise up this
generation of Youth who will truly deny
themselves, take up their cross and follow
You.  We declare that they are ones who will
count the cost and go all in after You.  Jesus, we
ask that they would be ones who will completely
lose their lives that they may gain them for all of
eternity.  We declare that they are ones who will
be willing to lose the whole world that they may
gain their souls.  We declare that this is a
generation who will be willing to offend the
whole world that they may not offend You.
Father, we ask that they would be mindful of the
things of God, not the things of man.  We
declare that these are ones who will not care
what anyone else says and will be willing to be
rejected by everyone else knowing You will
never reject them.

(Matthew 16:23-27)

## NO HINDRANCE

In Jesus' name we declare that there is no
hindrance over this generation from coming to
You! Father, we ask that You would teach the
youth how to prepare a way for You, to make
straight the path for You to come and invade this
generation. Father, would You teach us how to
lead the youth to the King, so they can find You,
so that every hindrance would be done away
with. We declare that this is a generation who
will find You. We declare that the hindrance of
possessions and the love of possessions will come
off them right now in Jesus' name! Father, we
ask that they would so long to follow after You
that no cost would be too great, but that they
would eagerly sell everything that they have that
they might be made perfect, then come and
follow You. We declare that this is a generation
who will give You everything and be the ones
who will sit on thrones with You in Your
Kingdom, judging with You. We declare that
they will be the ones who leave everything for
Your names sake, receiving a hundredfold back,
and eternal life, in Jesus' name!

(Matthew 19;13-15, Matthew 19:16-22,
Matthew 19:28-30, Matthew 3:3, Matthew 7:13-14)

# ENDURANCE

Thank You Jesus for Your Spirit on the youth. Thank You that You have not forgotten them. Each one of their names is engraved on the palm of Your hands. Thank You Jesus, that they don't need to search for acceptance from man or from the world, because You have already chosen and accepted them through Jesus. Lord, would You teach them to do all things without complaining and arguing, that they may be blameless and innocent children of God without blemish in the midst of a crooked and perverse generation among whom they shine as lights in the world, holding forth the word of life, so that in the day of Christ they might rejoice that they have not run or laboured in vain, in Jesus' name. Don't let these be the ones who fall away or are deceived or become offended because of You and Your righteous judgments, Jesus, but let them know You as a man of love and justice; which go hand in hand. Let them be proud of their Jesus who is coming to judge the world in righteousness and truth. Let them be the ones who follow the Lamb wherever He goes; who will not defile themselves with lust. May the youth of this generation be redeemed from mankind as first-fruits for God and the Lamb, and in their mouths no lie will be found, for they are blameless. Fill them with the love of Christ.

(Isaiah 49:16, Ephesians 1:4-6, Philippians 2:14-16, Matthew 24:10, Matthew 11:6, Psalm 101:1, Acts 17:31, Psalm 98:9, Revelation 14:4-5, Ephesians 3:19)

DAY 167

# PEACE

Thank You God for each one of the youth and how You have made them. Continue to mold each one into the image of Your Son! Holy Spirit, we pray that You would comfort each one's heart and that they would be at rest in You and have a desire to love You well. Jesus, Your word says, "Peace I leave with you; My peace I give you. Not as the world gives do I give to you." Jesus, we pray that the peace which surpasses all understanding would guard their hearts and minds through Christ Jesus our Lord. Let their hearts not be troubled nor let them be afraid. Jesus, You said that You would go away, but that You WILL return! Let each one rejoice in what You have done and that YOU ARE coming back for a pure and spotless bride! You went to be with the Father and now You are sitting at His right hand, interceding for each youth by name. Thank You that You went through all the pain for us; You died, rose again, and continue to serve by interceding for Your children! Thank You! May Your Kingdom come and Your will be done here on earth as it is in heaven! Thank You that You will give us the daily bread we need to live. Every morning You will pour out revelation and little treasures, so we can survive on the true Bread of Life!

(Isaiah 64:8, Genesis 1:27, John 14:26-28, Philippians 4:6-7, Ephesians 5:26-27, Hebrews 7:25, Romans 8:34, Matthew 16:21, Matthew 6:10, Jeremiah 29:11-14, Deuteronomy 8:3)

# INTEGRITY

Jesus, we ask that You ekballo teachers into the midst of the youth, so that they can teach them what is good, and so they may encourage the young women to love their families, to be self controlled, pure, homemakers, kind and submissive to those in authority over them, so that Your message will not be slandered. Father, in the same way, please ekballo teachers who will encourage the young men to be self-controlled in everything, that the young men would make themselves an example of good works with integrity and dignity in what they are teaching others through word and behaviour. LORD, may the youth carry a message that is sound beyond reproach, so that the opponent will be ashamed, having nothing to say about them or their teachers. Father, we go so far as to ask that this be translated into the workplace and schools as well. We ask that Your Spirit would teach them to be submissive to their bosses and educators in everything, and to be well-pleasing, not talking back or stealing, but demonstrating utter faithfulness, so that they may adorn the teaching of God our Saviour in everything. For Your grace appeared on that cross with salvation for all of mankind, teaching us and empowering us to deny godlessness and worldly passions and to live in a sensible, righteous and godly way in the present age, while we wait for the blessed hope and appearing of the glory of our great Saviour, Jesus Christ! Amen!

(Titus 2:1-14)

# LIGHT

Thank You Jesus, for the youth that will rise up and be a vast army of life and healing for the Kingdom of God.  Let them be the salt of the earth that causes others to thirst for You and let them be the city on a hill that cannot be hidden. Let the youth, together, be a light that shines, so that all may see their good works and give glory to You, Father!  In this time when the voice of the youth is being called out, let them be the voice of truth and not be ashamed of You, Jesus, but proclaim Your glory throughout the earth. Let them stand before kings and governors as a testimony to them of Your goodness.  RISE UP YOUTH!  Arise and shine for your light has come and the glory of the LORD has risen upon you.  Even when darkness covers the earth and thick darkness the people, LORD You will arise upon the youth and Your glory will be seen upon them! Nations shall come to their light and kings to the brightness of their rising.  Then the youth shall see and be radiant; their hearts shall thrill and exult, because the abundance of the sea shall be turned to them and the wealth of the nations shall come to them to build Your kingdom.  In Jesus' name.  Let it be!

(Isaiah 60:1-5, Ezekiel 37:10, Matthew 5:13-16, Matthew 10:18, Romans 1:16)

DAY 170

# SHINE

Father, we ask that the youth would come to You, that those who are thirsty would come to the water, to come and buy and drink Your wine and Your milk without money and without cost. Abba, we ask that this generation would no longer spend money for what does not fill or satisfy, but we declare that they will be ones who listen carefully to You, eat what is good and delight in Your abundance. Father, we ask that they will incline their ear and come to You and that as they hear You their souls shall live. The covenant that You have made with them is an everlasting covenant! Abba, thank You that this is a generation that other nations who don't even know them will run to because of You, because You have glorified them. Abba, we declare that they will be so in You, so taken by You, so glorified in You, that people from all over will run to them to find the King! We declare that this generation will so shine You that multitudes will be drawn to You through them. We declare that this is a generation that will seek You while You may be found, and call upon You while You are yet near. We declare that they will forsake every wicked way and every unrighteous thought and return to You. You promise that You will have mercy on them and will abundantly pardon them when they repent. We declare that they will seek You and so find You that the multitudes will be drawn to You through them, in Jesus' name!

(Isaiah 55:1-7)

# DISCIPLINE

Abba, You are a good Father, and a good father
disciplines his kids.  Holy Spirit, would You
reveal to the youth the true love of the Father!
You have not given the youth a spirit of fear, but
of power, love, self-discipline, and a sound
mind.  Help the youth receive correction well,
and know they do not have to be afraid.  Show
them Your true heart behind it, so they can
become true sons and daughters of the living
God!  In Jesus name we pray, amen.

(1 Timothy 1:7, Hebrews 12:6-8)

# IDENTITY

Jesus, we ask that the Spirit of the Lord would be on the youth because You have anointed them to preach the gospel to the poor. You have sent them to bind up the brokenhearted, to proclaim liberty to the captives and the opening of the prison to those who are bound, to proclaim the year of the Lord's favor, to give them a beautiful headdress instead of ashes, the oil of gladness instead of mourning, the garment of praise instead of a faint spirit. May they be called oaks of righteousness, the planting of the Lord, that You may be glorified. We declare that the youth will rebuild the ancient ruins; that they shall raise up the former devastation. The youth shall repair the ruined cities, the devastations of many generations. Instead of their shame, they shall have a double portion; instead of dishonor they shall rejoice in their lot. Therefore, in their land, they shall possess a double portion; they shall have everlasting joy. All who see them shall acknowledge that they are an offspring the Lord has blessed. Let them greatly rejoice in the Lord. Let their souls exult in their God, for You have clothed them with garments of salvation. You have covered them with the robe of righteousness like a bride and a bridegroom are adorned. Jesus, would You cause righteousness and praise to sprout up before all the nations through the youth. In Jesus' name.

(Isaiah 61)

# GODLINESS

Jesus, we pray for leaders who agree with the sound doctrine of our LORD Jesus Christ and with the teaching that promotes godliness to encompass the youth; leaders who are humble, full of understanding, that are able to settle fights and bring genuine peace. LORD, may the youth understand and withdraw from those having a sick interest in disputes and arguments over words for from these things come envy, quarreling, slander, evil suspicions, and constant disagreement among people whose minds are deprived of truth; who imagine that godliness is a way to material gain. But LORD, may the youth of this generation understand that godliness with contentment is gain! Abba, the youth did not bring anything into this world and cannot take anything out of it, so may the treasures that they seek be ones of eternal value which are people! Please keep them safe from the temptations of money, knowing that the love of it is the root of all kinds of evil; those who crave it have even fallen away from the faith and pierced themselves with many pains. Holy Spirit, please teach them to run from these things and to pursue righteousness, godliness, faith, love, endurance and gentleness. Please teach them how to fight the good fight of faith; taking hold of eternal life that they have been called to. May Your grace abound in them more and more each day! In Jesus name, amen.

(1 Timothy 6:3-12)

# LEADERS

Jesus, we thank You for this upcoming
generation which will be one that will not despise
their youth, but the youth will set for the
believers an example in speech, in conduct, in
love, in faith, and purity. May each one devote
themselves to the public reading of scripture, to
exhortation, to teaching. May they not neglect
the gift they have, which was given to them by
prophecy when the council of elders laid their
hands on them. May each one practice these
things, immersing themselves in them, so that all
may see You. Let each youth keep a close watch
on themselves and on their teaching, that they
would persist in this, for by so doing they will
save both themselves and their hearers.

(1Timothy 4:12-16)

## HOLINESS

Father, we declare that this is a generation of Josiahs, who will turn to You with all their heart, soul and might, unlike any other generation has ever done before. We declare that this is a generation who will pursue after Your heart, understand the purity and holiness of God, and passionately destroy anything that defiles or hinders. Father, we ask that they would be ones who will get rid of anything dedicated to any other god besides You. Father, would You give them a sensitivity to recognize what is good and what is evil. We declare that they are ones who will hate everything that defiles, and will love You purely and wholly; that whatever You love they would love, what brings You joy would bring them great joy, that keeping Your commandments would be their delight!

(2 Kings 23:4, 2 Kings 23:25, 1 John 5:3, Hebrews 5:14)

# SELFLESSNESS

Father, we declare over the youth that they will
be of one heart and one mind. Father, we ask
that You would raise them up to be ones who
don't even care about possessions, but would
gladly sell everything they have to follow You
and share it all with one another, not counting
anything their own. Father, thank You that they
are ones who will give witness to the resurrection
of Jesus with great power. We decree great
grace over them! We decree that they are ones
who will not love their own lives, even when
faced with death, but would gladly lay down their
lives for the gospel and for one another.

(Acts 5:32-33, Revelation 12:11, John 15:13)

# ENCOUNTER

Abba, draw the youth to Your heart, by the
power of Your love.  Let them hear You
knocking on the door of their heart, so that You
will come in and eat with them and they with
You.  Come on Jesus.  Let the power of Your
love fill them, O God.  That everyone would
know that the youth belong to You because of
their radical, self-sacrificial love.  Greater love
has no man than this: that a man lay down his life
for his friend.  Jesus, You laid down Your life for
the youth while they were still sinners and
enemies of God.  Draw the youth to Your heart,
so that they would be those who You will call
Your friends.  Let them walk in Your love that is
filled with power and life.  Let them be ones who
will carry the true gospel to the ends of the earth;
Your gospel that is the power of God for
salvation.  Let them not be ashamed of it or of
You, Jesus.  Let them be captivated by Your
beauty and holiness just like the creatures and
elders in heaven are, who day and night do not
cease to cry out, "Holy, Holy, Holy is the Lord
God Almighty, who was and is and is to come."
Let them be holy as You are holy Jesus,
righteous as You are righteous and pure as You
are pure.  Let them cast their crowns at Your
feet, Jesus and count every treasure on earth as
dung for the great worth of knowing You.
Everyone who is in You must live as You did
Jesus, so let these be ones who will be little
Christs on earth and through whom Your love
can move.  Let these be ones who abide in You

and have confidence in You, so that they will not shrink away from You in shame at Your coming, Jesus. Let them be ones who watch and are ready for their King to return. For the glory of Your name Jesus. All for the King of Kings! Jesus, let these be ones who will do everything they can to get wisdom, though it costs them everything they have.

(Revelation 3:20, John 13:35, John 15:13, Romans 5:8, John 15:15, Revelation 4:8-11, 1 Peter 1:15-16, Philippians 3:8-11, 1 John 2:5-6, 1 John 2:28-29, Acts 11:26, Matthew 24, 42-47, Proverbs 4:7)

# PURITY

LORD, we pray for the youth that they would be able to pay attention to Your wisdom; that they would listen closely to Your understanding, so that they may maintain discretion and their lips safeguard knowledge. Father, send heavenly hosts around the youth as guards to protect them from the forbidden woman whose lips drip honey and her words are smoother than oil. LORD, You said that in the end she is as bitter as wormwood and as sharp as a double edged sword. Protect them from treading where her feet tread because they go down to death! Her steps head straight for Sheol! That snake does not consider the path of life, and all who tread where she walks do not know that her ways are unstable. So Abba, fine tune the ears of the youth to hear the Truth. Jesus You are the Way, the Truth and the Life. Send help so that they will not turn away from the words of Your mouth. Keep them FAR away from her and prevent them from going near the door of her house, otherwise, they will give up their vitality to others and their years to someone cruel; strangers will drain their resources, and their earnings will end up in a foreigner's house. Abba, please keep this generation from being consumed because of a lack of discipline and correction. We say no to this rebellion and ask for a rising up of youth who would agree with You that Your discipline and correction bring life! Pour out Your great grace to help them obey godly teachers and mentors and keep them from complete ruin as has happened to so many before them. LORD, we proclaim that this generation will so deeply love You that they will stir Your heart and cause it to skip a beat. We proclaim that this generation will remove the stumbling blocks from the feet of the people, so that they can run to You. We proclaim that this is the glorious year of the LORD's favour and today is the day of salvation!

(Proverbs 5:1-14, Song of Solomon 4:9, Isaiah 57:14, Luke 4:19, 2 Corinthians 6:2)

## REVIVAL

Jesus, the youth have heard of Your fame and they have heard of Your deeds also. Let them stand in awe of them. We thank You for the signs and wonders that have been done and the hearts that have been touched. Abba, would you do it again please; do it in our day, in our time make them known. In your wrath, remember Your mercy! Send revival in this day and age. They heard what You have done; let them search it in Your word; let the heart of God be made known. The wrath of God is coming upon this earth again, so Lord would You prepare the hearts of the children, so that they will not be offended when the judgments come upon the earth. Let them seek You now. Do not forget Your mercy O God. Holy Spirit, would You remind the youth of the teachings of Jesus and may they be thankful in every season. Whether in plenty or in hunger, in abundance or in need, in suffering and in persecution. Lord, would they know they can do all things through Christ who strengthens them!

(Habakkuk 3, John 14:26, Philippians 4:12-13)

# ETERNITY

Thank You Jesus for the youth that will come boldly before Your throne of grace, that they may find mercy and grace to help in their time of need. Jesus would You give them an eternal perspective, that they would see what is true and what will just fade away. All people are like grass, and their beauty is like a flower of the field that will fade away. The grass withers and the flowers fade, but the word of the Lord remains forever. Let this generation sell the things that have no value and buy the pearl of great price! We pray the youth will be in complete surrender and draw near to You, God!

(Hebrews 4:16, Isaiah 40:6-8, Matthew 13:45-46, James 4:7-8)

# CHARACTER

Jesus, thank You that Your divine power has granted to the youth all things that pertain to life and godliness, through the knowledge of You who called them to Your own glory and excellence. You have granted to them Your precious and very great promises, so that through them, the youth may become partakers of the divine nature, having escaped from the corruption that is in the world because of sinful desire. For this very reason, help them make every effort to supplement their faith with virtue, and virtue with knowledge, and knowledge with self-control, to self-control with steadfastness, and steadfastness with godliness, and godliness with brotherly affection, and brotherly affection with love. For if these qualities are in them and are increasing, they keep the youth from being ineffective or unfruitful in the knowledge of our Lord Jesus Christ. LORD we know that whoever lacks these qualities is so nearsighted that he is blind, having forgotten that he was cleansed from his former sins. Therefore, teach the youth to be all the more diligent to make their calling and election sure, for if they practice these qualities they will never fall. For in this way they will be richly provided for with an entrance into the eternal kingdom of our Lord and Savior Jesus Christ.

(2 Peter 1:3-11)

# HOLINESS

Father, we ask that the youth could be the ones who will cry out, "Build up! Build up! Prepare the way! Take the stumbling block out of the way of God's people!" Father, may they be the ones to prepare a way for You. LORD remove these last stumbling blocks, so that this generation can return to You. Abba, use them for Your Kingdom and Your glory. O God, we recognize that You are the High and Lofty One, who inhabits eternity, whose name is HOLY. Father, You dwell in the high and holy place along with those who are of a contrite and humble spirit. We decree humility over the youth that they will be ones who recognize their need for You and are broken & contrite before You, because those are the ones that You can dwell with! Abba, we want this generation to be the ones that You can dwell in and not have to leave because of sin! We decree a reviving over this generation as they humble themselves before You! We decree that this is a generation of holiness, because without holiness no one can see You.

(Isaiah 57:14-15, Hebrews 12:14)

# REPENTANCE

O LORD, may Your youth who are called by Your name, humble themselves and pray and seek Your face and turn from their wicked ways; then You will hear from heaven and You will forgive their sins and bring healing to the places they reside.  LORD, we thank You that regardless of what people have done, that as soon as they turn to You and walk away from that which opposes You, that You are quick to forgive and turn Your eyes and open Your ears and give attention to them when they pray. LORD, we are asking that You mark this generation and consecrate them; that Your name be with them forever and that Your eyes and heart be with them forever.  May they walk as King David walked and be called youth after God's own heart.

(2 Chronicle 7:14-17, Acts 13:22)

# OVERCOMERS

Father, we decree that the youth will not give up in tribulation, but will continue in the faith, recognizing that they must go through many tribulations to enter the kingdom of God. Father, we ask that they would be ones who will proclaim Your word with boldness! We ask that they would not take offense even if spoken against by those who don't believe, but that they will continue to speak boldly in the Lord. We pray that they would make room for You to confirm the word of Your grace with signs and wonders. Would You set their faces like flint to not give up no matter what comes against them. We ask that they will be so grounded in You, that they will not be lead astray either by praise or persecution, but will give You all the honour and all the glory. We declare that they are ones who will rise up again even if left for dead, and will continue to speak Your Word without fear. Father, we thank You that even in the midst of persecution, this will be a generation who will be filled with joy and the Holy Spirit. May You use them as overcomers who will not love their lives even in front of death, but will so love You and love their neighbour that they would rather lay down their lives that others might live, that as they lose their lives now, they will save them for all of eternity. We decree that this is a generation that will endure to the end and be saved, in Jesus' name.

(Acts 13:50-52, Acts 14:1-22, Isaiah 50:7,
Revelation 12:11, John 12:25, 1 John 3:16)

# ADOPTION

Thank You Jesus for calling the youth out of darkness and into Your marvelous light. Thank You that You have not given them a spirit of bondage to fear, but You have given them the Spirit of adoption by whom they cry out, "Abba, Father!" Let them live according to the Spirit of God and set their minds on the things of the Spirit in Jesus' name. Teach them to call and draw Your kingdom to come on earth as it is in heaven. Thank You Jesus. Thank You that You have not given them a spirit of fear, but of power and of love and of a sound mind. God, let them walk in the boldness, love and power that You have available to them and not back down, but know that the God of Hosts is on their side and You will never leave them. In Jesus' name.

(1 Peter 2:9, Romans 8:15, Romans 8:5, 1 Timothy 1:7, Matthew 6:10, Ephesians 1:19, Deuteronomy 31:6, Matthew 28:20)

# THANKFULNESS

Jesus, we thank You for each one of the youth and thank You that You are willing to pour out Your revelation on the youth. In Your word it says in the last days that Your sons and daughters will prophesy and Your old men will dream dreams and Your young men will see visions. So Jesus, we thank You for continually wanting and desiring to pour out Your Spirit on ALL flesh! God, we are asking for a group of youth that will be on fire for You and Your name's sake. Let them be continually grateful and faithful in the little things, that they may be thankful with the much! In Exodus, there was a group of Israelites who were wandering in the desert and You provided meals to test their hearts to see if they would obey You. Jesus, as You test the youth and refine them into the youth You have designed and desired them to be, Lord, we are asking that they would be found faithful and true to You Jesus, that they would be a grateful people after Your own heart. Allow them to see the little blessings in life, knowing that if they will be faithful with the small things, then they will be faithful with the much larger things.

(Exodus 16:4, Joel 2:28-29, Acts 2:17-18, Luke 16:10)

# WORSHIP

Father, we thank You for the youth!!! Jesus, we ask that they would be the ones who, in the midst of the worst pain and persecution, even while bound for Your name, would be praising You day and night!!! We decree a praise to arise from this generation that will be so pure and holy; worship in Spirit and truth; that the suddenlies will come as the youth worship. Father, we ask that they could praise You so well that others who are in chains would hear them and be drawn to You. Father, thank You for the suddenlies of God coming; that the very foundations of prison and darkness would shake as they praise You. We decree that as this generation worships, their own chains will fall off, but not only theirs, but also those of the people around them. We decree a worship that will wage war in the heavenlies, that the multitudes will be liberated simply by their worship! We decree that they will not worship for any gain they can get from it, but that they will lay aside their own desires. We pray that when You call the youth to certain locations that they will not want to leave when it is hard, but instead will stay, so that whole families may be saved! Father, we ask that the testimony of their selfless worship would draw those who persecute them and their whole families to be saved!!! We decree that this is a generation that people will run to, asking, "What must I do to be saved?" Father, we ask that You would give them the answer to know what to say to see true salvation come; "Believe on the Lord Jesus Christ, and you will be saved, you and your whole household." We ask that in each unique situation, You would give them an answer from heaven. Father, teach them how to speak the word of the Lord that will allow people to hear and be saved. Thank You for complete turnaround situations, where praise in persecution results in the salvation and baptism of the persecutors and their whole houses. Those who once persecuted them will instead be washing their feet and serving them. From persecution, we pray, would come fellowship meals and unity with new believers and great joy!!!

(Acts 16:25-34)

## LABOURERS

LORD, may the youth from this region so know and encounter You that You would be able to ekballo them into the harvest field. We pray that You would give these ones a voice in their local churches to reason with them from the scriptures, explaining and showing the love and power of God. May they be able to persuade those who truly fear God. Protect them from those that may become jealous and desire to cause trouble.

(Acts 17:1-5)

# IDENTITY

Jesus, we thank You that in You the Youth are already accepted, so they do not have to strive to find love or acceptance anywhere else. Thank You that even before they were born, You predestined each one individually to be adopted into Your family. Thank You Jesus that You have lavished Your grace on them in all wisdom and insight. Thank You that You have chosen them; hand picked them to be holy and blameless before You in love. Thank You that Your grace brings salvation to all people and trains them to renounce ungodliness and worldly passions, and to live self-controlled, upright and godly lives in the present age. Let them be ones who wait for the blessed hope and the appearing of the glory of our great God and Savior Jesus Christ. Thank You Jesus that You gave Yourself up for each one of them, redeeming them from all lawlessness and to purify them for Yourself as a people for Your own possession who are zealous for good works.

(Ephesians 1:3-10, Titus 2:11-14)

# TRUE RELIGION

Thank You Jesus for the youth. Thank You that You are good to those who wait for You, to the person who seeks You. Jesus, we ask that You would teach them to be quick to listen and slow to speak. Jesus, would You show the youth what true religion is; that it is looking after the widows and the orphans, the ones that don't know You yet, and keep themselves unstained from the world. Keep them pure O God, keep them safe. May they dwell beneath the shadow of Your wings. Thank You that You are their Rock and their Salvation, their very present help in times of trouble. Let each one be sealed for redemption, we pray. Amen!

(Lamentation 2:25-26, James 1:19, James 1:26-27, Psalm 17:8, Psalm 62:5-7, Ephesians 1:13)

# HOLINESS

Abba, You are glorious!!!  Father, we give You all the honor and glory and praise today!  May Your name be lifted high and glorified!  May Your name be exalted!  We declare that we will bring glory to Your name and praise You forever and ever!!!  You are great and Your greatness is unsearchable!  Father, we ask that You would raise up this generation to know who You really are; to know You in all Your glory, holiness, splendor, mercy, compassion, justice, righteousness, wonder, and goodness.  Abba, may they see the truth of who Jesus is and so study the real One that no counterfeit will have any pull on them.  We declare that these are ones who will know the height to which You, the One High and Lifted Up, have called them and will walk with You in heavenly places, counting themselves dead to all sin and alive to God in Christ Jesus.  We decree that the youth are a  people who will believe that it is possible to live holy before You, and will be a truly pure and spotless bride.  We declare that this generation will not water down the gospel, but will believe that it is the power of God to full salvation for everyone who believes.  We decree that this is a generation of great faith unlike You have ever seen before.  Abba, may this be the generation that ushers in Your Kingdom saying with the Spirit, "Come Lord Jesus, come!"

(Psalm 145:1-3, Mark 13:21-22, Ephesians 2:6, Romans 6:11, 1 Peter 1:15, Ephesians 5:27, Romans 1:16, Luke 7:9, Revelation 22:17)

# PURITY

LORD, may this generation no longer collect for themselves treasures on earth, where moth and rust destroy and where thieves break in and steal. May they collect for themselves treasures in heaven. For where the treasure of the youth is, there their heart is also. Create a clean heart in them, O God, and renew a faithful spirit within the youth. May they seek You for this and cry aloud until You have responded with favour. LORD, sprinkle clean water on the youth and cleanse them from everything that grieves Your heart. When the youth have cried out to You, we pray that You will respond with, "I will give you a new heart and put a new spirit in you. I will remove your stubborn hearts and give you obedient hearts. I will put My Spirit in you. I will enable you to live by My laws and you will obey My rules. Then you will live in the land that I gave your ancestors. You will be My people, and I will be your God." LORD, do this for Your name's sake, so that Your name will be made famous once more in this region and in this nation. LORD, may the youth in our region rise up and set the standard of God for this generation. May they be the ones You prophesied about saying, "I will pour out My spirit upon all flesh and your sons and your daughters shall prophesy."

(Matthew 6:19-21, Psalm 51:10, Ezekiel 36:25-28, Joel 2:28)

DAY 193

# HARVEST

Jesus, we thank You for youth who are grabbing
a hold of Your heart and Your vision and
running with it. Thank You for those youth who
are already stepping up and calling down Your
kingdom to come on earth as it is in heaven.
Thank You for those who are hearing Your
heartbeat and laying down the plumbline of God
in their schools and spheres of influence. Jesus,
we ask right now that You would encourage
them, that they would not grow weary in doing
good, but that they would know that they will
reap a harvest if they do not give up. Thank
You, Jesus, that You promise that those who
sow in tears shall reap with shouts of joy; that the
one who goes out weeping shall come home with
shouts of joy, bringing their sheaves with them.
Jesus, let them see the joy and privilege of loving
You and being carriers of the gospel. Let them
keep Your commandments and abide in Your
love just as You keep Your Father's
commandments and abide in His love!

(Amos 7:8, Galatians 6:9, Psalm 126:5, John 15:10-11)

## SEEK

Jesus, there are some pretty dark times that will be coming on the face of this earth and the youth need to be prepared. Jesus, we are asking You to remember in Your mercy they are but a breath. Let the youth seek You now while there is still time before the destruction and plagues increase upon the face of this earth. Show them the urgency that is needed and the hour they are in. Let them begin to hunger and thirst for righteousness now, for then they will be filled and they will not faint from thirst or hunger in adversity. Keep their hearts warm. May they repent, so times of refreshing may come.

(Amos 8:1-13, Psalm 39:4-5, Matthew 5:6, Matthew 24:12-13, Act 3:19)

# PRAYER

Father, we ask that You would teach the youth how to pray. God, would You put a cry in their hearts to ask You for this. ABBA, would You teach them to pray in such a way that shifts atmospheres and causes prisons to shake and chains to fall off. Teach them to pray and to stand in the gap for a whole nation and generation and see them saved because one person said yes to seeking You in the secret place. Teach them to pray with such passion and persistence that they will not give up even if nothing appears to be changing. Teach them to seek You until they find You. Teach them to intercede and to hit the mark every time. Teach them to pray in such a way that others see the truth and are saved. Teach them to pray to see the sick healed and the dead raised, even if they have to press in for it!!! Abba, teach them to intercede until they see the bowls in heaven tipped out over an entire nation. Jesus, teach this generation to be the ones who pray WITHOUT CEASING. Teach them to pray with passion in the secret place, where fancy words don't matter and they don't care about being seen by men. Teach them to pray so powerfully that the places that they are in shake, and all of them are filled with the Holy Spirit and go out speaking Your word in boldness.

(Ezekiel 22:30, Matthew 7:7, Matthew 6:5-13,
Luke 11:1, Acts 4:24, Acts 4:31, Acts 16:25-26,
Luke 18:1-8, 1 John 5:16, 1 Kings 17:17-24,
Revelation 5:8, 1 Thessalonians 5:17)

DAY 196

# ARISE

Jesus, we thank You for each youth and that
You have made them all to be mighty men and
women of God who will love You well!  Jesus,
David was only a youth when You anointed him
as king; Gideon was tearing down idols in his
father's house; and Jeremiah was declaring Your
word to the nations.  These youth are not too
young, in fact, You enjoy using children as
You've said, "Do not  hinder the children from
coming, for such belongs the kingdom of
heaven!"  So, would You do it again in our
time.  God, would You use the young ones to see
Your Kingdom come and Your will be done here
on earth as it is in heaven!  Abba, do not pass by
us; let us see Your glory!  In Jesus' name we pray
and thank You for all that You have done and all
that You have yet to do!

(1 Samuel 16:11, Judges 6:25-27a, Matthew 19:14,
Habakkuk 3:1)

# PERSECUTION

Jesus, we ask that You would teach the youth to fear You above the law. God, let them be honorable men and women who keep the law and honor the leaders of our nation, but let them fear You above men and the law. If they are in a compromising situation, we declare they will always choose to obey the law of God above the law of men. Jesus, teach them to fear You now, while it's easy, so that no matter how hard they are squashed, tested, persecuted and pressured they will say with boldness, "Whether it is right in the sight of God to listen to you rather than to God, you must judge, for we cannot but speak of what we have seen and heard." Jesus, teach them that being persecuted for Your name is a great joy and honor and You promised that it would happen, so don't let them be ones who cave under pressure. Abba, we ask that You would teach the youth Your truth so that, no matter what, they will not compromise in Jesus' name. Let them be ones who endure to the end and are saved. Let them run the race and win! Thank You Jesus that the youth in this generation are overcomers through the power of Your blood!

(Acts 4:19, Acts 5:41, Matthew 10:22, Matthew 5:11, 2 Timothy 3:12, 1 Corinthians 9:24, Romans 8:37, Revelation 12:11)

# AWAKENING

Jesus, thank You for each one of the youth.  Would You reveal Your truth to them, so that they may see Your heart!  Let them know Your will for their lives, because people without a vision perish.  Let them not be drunk with wine or be pulled away by things of this world, rather may they be filled with the Holy Spirit!  Jesus, for those who are struggling to overcome addictions or the things of this world, we are asking that salvation would come, that Your LOVE would fill each one.  Let them come lifting holy hands before You and singing psalms, hymns and spiritual songs.  Let the youth begin to gather and pray at school, so that they may see Your kingdom come there.  We pray that teachers will totally get rocked for the sake of the gospel and the cause of Christ!  We pray that prayer meetings and worship moments would erupt in schools, so that the glory of God may be made manifest.  We cry out for schools to be houses of prayer for all nations.  O God, stir students to come to school not because of the great academics and extracurricular activities, but rather because God, You showed up, made Yourself known and now people desire to come from all over the place to see what GOD is doing!  May each one bear much fruit; may they abide in You Abba.  In Jesus name, amen!!!

(Ephesians 5:18, Psalm 25:4-5, 2 Peter 3:9, Ephesians 5:18-19, 1 Thessalonians 5:11, 1Timothy 2:8, John 15:5-8, Mark 16:15)

# HOLINESS

Father, we ask that the youth would realize that You are a God who has emotions and is affected by us. Abba, may they not play down what their decisions do to You. Jesus, we ask that they would be ones who so love You that they would hate what You hate because they don't want to grieve You. Father, we ask that they would have a heart sold out towards You, that they would never grieve You. Make them ones who know Your holiness and hate everything that defiles and displeases You. Father, may they hear the warning sound of the trumpet and rise to the call, turning from all wickedness in true humility and repentance. Abba, we declare that these are ones who will go after Your holiness unashamedly and will be able to be used by You to usher in Your healing and Your outpouring on an entire nation! Abba, may they be pure and undefiled before You, so that You can give them the trumpet to make a clear sound that will raise up the warriors in holiness to go out and to see Your Kingdom come!!!

(Ezekiel 6:9, Ezekiel 5:11, 2 Chronicles 7:14, 1 Corinthians 14:8)

## TRAINING

Jesus, thank You that You are teaching these young ones from their youth, so that they will continue to walk in and declare Your righteous decrees when they are older. Holy Spirit, the only way to become pure is by living according to Your word, so would You remind them of the things they need to learn and walk out so that they can become that pure and spotless bride that You are looking for. Show them how to live a consecrated life to You; let none of the things of this world get in the way of Your right decrees O God! Help them to seek You first in all they do. In Jesus' name we pray, amen!

(Lamentations 3:27, Matthew 6:33, Psalm 119:9, Psalm 71:17)

# WATCHMEN

Abba, we thank You for the amazing youth. We are asking that You would specifically mark them to be watchmen on the wall in their generation. Thank You Jesus, that even now You are burning on specific hearts to rise up and sound the alarm, speaking out for righteousness and truth and warning the people of Your judgments. Whenever they hear a word from Your mouth, let them give the warning from You, so that lives might be saved. Jesus, we ask that You would train them in discernment and wisdom, that they would only speak when You say speak, but when You say speak, that they would not remain silent in Jesus' name. Let them be accustomed to the word of righteousness and become mature having their senses trained because of practice, to discern good and evil. Let them know Your voice clearly and let these be the watchmen on the walls who are never silent day or night. Thank You Jesus.

(Isaiah 62:6-7, Ezekiel 3:16-17, Hebrews 5:13-14, John 12:49)

## FEAR OF THE LORD

Father, we pray for a holy fear of God to come
upon the youth and may they cry out to You
knowing that Your faithfulness endures
forever. May they cry out to You in their distress
and may You then put them in spacious places.
God, we ask that Your grace and favour come
upon the youth in this hour and we thank You
for being there for them, so that they will not be
afraid. Abba, when they come into right
relationship with You, man will not be able to do
anything to them because You will be their
Helper. Abba, we pray that they will know that it
is better to take refuge in You than to trust in
their friends or people in positions of power,
because You will never fail them.

(Psalm 118:4-9)

# FOLLOWERS

Father, we ask that the youth would be ones who
will see through Your eyes. LORD, we ask that
in all the land that You have entrusted to them,
that they would be faithful to take away ALL its
detestable things and ALL its abominations.
Father, may this be a people who will value Your
presence enough to remove anything that grieves
You. Father, would You give them one heart
and put a new spirit within them, taking away all
hardness and giving them a heart of flesh. Abba,
may they walk in Your statutes and keep Your
judgments and do them, that then they may be
Your people and You will be their God. We ask
that their hearts would follow after You and not
after any detestable thing, but that what is
loathsome to You would be loathsome to them.
Father, may they so value You, that nothing on
earth has any hold of them; that they would
gladly lay everything down to follow You.

(Ezekiel 11:17-21, 1 John 2:15)

# SAVING GRACE

LORD, teach the youth to test the spirits that whisper thoughts and ideas to them. Teach them how to determine if they are from You or not, because many false voices have gone out into the world especially in this hour. LORD, awaken the youth to recognize the spirit of antichrist and lawlessness and empower them by Your grace to reject that which is contrary to Your heart! Abba, fill the youth with Your love, so that they can be empowered to love one another, for everyone who truly loves as You have declared in 1 Corinthians 13, has been born of You. LORD, the one who does not truly love does not really know You. Forgive them who cannot love because they have not received the revelation of You and cannot give what they do not have because You are love! LORD, Your greatest display of love was sacrificing Your Son, so that we could regain a relationship with You that was lost through corruption. Thank You for Your rich love for the Youth and the salvation of the cross.

(1 John 4:1, 1 John 4:7-9)

# HONOUR

Jesus, thank You for the youth. Jesus, we ask
that You would teach them to honor
extravagantly. No matter how culture and
society define young people, we ask that these be
ones who will honor their parents, grandparents,
their teachers and outdo one another in showing
honor. Teach them how to show respect to
everyone, even those who mistreat them. Let
them truly raise the bar and set the example for
believers in their speech, in their conduct, their
life, in the way they love, in their great faith in
You and in the untainted purity that they exhibit.
We declare that the youth are not defined or
limited to what culture defines them as, but they
will rise up and be the mighty men and women of
God who slay the enemy for the kingdom of
God. Let them be ones like Eleazar who rise up
and fight until their hands are weary and cling to
the sword. Lord, use them to bring about a great
victory in that day. May they be like Benaiah,
who was a doer of great deeds, who snatched the
enemy's spear out of his hand and used it to slay
the enemy. Or may they be like the three chief
mighty men who risked their lives to honor and
serve their king. Thank You Jesus for this
valiant army that You are raising up; an army
who will fight through honor, praise and love.

(Romans 12:10, Ephesians 6:2, Proverbs 17:6,
1 Timothy 4:12, 2 Samuel 23:8-39)

## MARKED

Jesus, we thank You for Your very great and precious promises in Your word.  We thank You that the youth will humble themselves and walk before You, so that Your plans and purposes can come to pass in their lifetime!  Jesus, You have called the youth to be holy in Your sight and seek Your kingdom first.  Thank You that the youth are marked with a seal; the promised Holy Spirit; a deposit guaranteeing their inheritance until the redemption of those who are Your possession- to the praise of Your glory.  Amen.

(Deuteronomy 11:22-23, 1 Peter 1:16, Matthew 6:33, Ephesians 4:10, Ephesians 1:13-14)

# BLESSING

Jesus, thank You for the call that You have on each one of the youth.  Thank You that in this hour the youth are truly rising up boldly for Your kingdom and Your glory.  Jesus, we ask that these would have the grace and discernment to be ones who will not walk in the counsel of the ungodly, nor stand in the way of sinners, nor sit in the seat of scoffers, but let their delight be in Your law; that day and night they would meditate on it, in Jesus' name.  We declare that they will be like trees planted by streams of water that bear their fruit in due season, whose leaves will not wither, and who will prosper in everything that they do, for the glory of Your name.  Jesus, we ask that each of them would know for themselves how lovely Your dwelling place is, O Lord of hosts!  Let their souls love and even faint for the courts of the Lord; let their heart and flesh sing for joy to the living God.  We declare that these are blessed because they will dwell in Your house and will forever be singing Your praise!  They are blessed because their strength will be in You.  As they go through the Valley of Baca (weeping) they will make it a place of springs, as they go from strength to strength.  For You, Lord God, are a sun and shield; You bestow favor and honor.  No good thing do You withhold from those who walk uprightly.  O Lord of hosts, blessed are the youth when they trust in You!  Do it Jesus for Your glory and Your kingdom!

(Psalm 1:1-3, Psalm 84)

## IDENTITY

Abba, thank You that You have chosen this generation as Your own. You have marked and chosen a people to be holy and blameless before You. Open the eyes of our youth to know that You have already accepted them, Jesus, and that they do not have to strive to "fit in" or be beautiful or accepted. Would You reveal that truth right now. Would You fill this generation with such radical love and boldness that it doesn't matter what other people say to or about them, that it could never shake their identity. Jesus, Your identity was never defined by man. Even though You were fully man, the Father always defined who You were. Spirit of Revelation, reveal the Father's radical, powerful love to the youth, that they would know and live out their identity in You. Amen.

(Ephesians 1:4-6, John 15:16)

## CHOSEN

Thank You Jesus for these fiery ones!  Open
their eyes to see You in Your beauty, to see You
in Your glory, to see Your eyes that are like
flames of fire.  Thank You Jesus that You have
chosen the youth, and that You have called them
out of the darkness and into the marvelous light!
Thank You that You have called this generation
to proclaim the good news.  Once they were not
a people, but now You have called them Your
very own.  You have shown them mercy, Lord,
now  pour out Your abundant grace.  Show our
youth how much You love them and how You
have been longing for the day when they will run
into Your arms!  We pray a blessing on their
families.  Draw them all close to Your heart and
let Your liquid love encounter them!  Bless each
one, draw each one, and encounter each one.
Blow our minds because of the good work You
are doing in our generation!  Abba, thank You
for making each one!  You're amazing, Jesus!

(1 Peter 2:9, John 6:44, Luke 15:20)

## SONSHIP

Father, it was Your good pleasure to crush Jesus, so that we could come to know You. Your promise was that when Jesus bore the sin of the world He would see His offspring. Father, we pray that this generation would become Jesus' offspring. Show the youth how to run after You, to seek You and to call out to You. We pray that You would reveal Yourself to an entire generation, so that they may know how real You are!

(Isaiah 53:10, Hebrews 11:6)

# LOVE

Thank You that You have chosen this
generation before the foundation of the world
that we should be holy and without blame before
You in love.  You predestined a people to
adoption as Your children, according to the
good pleasure of Your will, to the praise and
glory of Your grace.  You accepted us in the
Beloved, in whom we have redemption, the
forgiveness of sins, according to the riches of
Your grace which You made to abound toward
us in all wisdom and prudence.  Would You
make known to this generation, Abba, the
mystery of Your will, according to Your good
pleasure which You purposed in Yourself.
Abba, we ask would You raise up youth in our
generation who will seek after wisdom and
search for it even though it costs everything they
have.  Give them the hunger and persistence to
seek for You and find You when they search for
You with all of their hearts.  Thank You Jesus,
for Your incredible love.  Reveal Your love to
our youth, that they can understand the height,
width, depth and length of it and be filled with all
the fullness of God.  Thank You Jesus.  We call
this generation into Your kingdom in Jesus'
name.  Amen.

(Ephesians 1:4-9, Proverbs 4:7, Proverbs 18:15,
Jeremiah 29:13, Ephesians 3:14-21)

# ENCOUNTER

Father, we ask that this would be a generation
that would seek Your glory!!! That the youth
would be true in You, with no unrighteousness in
them. Father, we ask that You would encounter
the youth, that they would be radically saved and
set on fire for You. Father, we are asking for an
incredible thirsting for You, that they would
come to You and drink, and believe in You, that
out of their hearts would flow rivers of living
water. Father, we ask that they would believe in
You that they might receive the Holy
Spirit!!! Be glorified, O God!!! Jesus we're
asking that eyes would be opened and that this
generation would believe You and be
saved! May they cry out to You like the jailer,
"What must I do to be saved?" and then do
whatever You say! Father, would You send
those around them at the perfect time, just like
You sent Ananias to Paul, to be able to pray for
them. Father, would You send those who will
speak out what You see, and not what the world
sees, and will pray for this entire generation, and
contend for the youth, until they come into the
fullness of God!!! May they know that they are
loved by You and Your people!!!

(John 7:18, John 7:37-39, Acts 9:15-18)

# PROCLAMATION

Thank You Jesus that You are the Lover of our souls. Father, we pray that You would enrapture the youth with Your love, that Your kindness would draw them to repentance. Thank You for the mandate that You have on their lives, that they are Your messengers. Abba, would You plant Your word inside each one so deeply and so passionately that even if they try to contain it, that they won't be able to because Your hand is upon them. Your word is like fire inside their bones that they cannot contain. Thank You for the message that You are giving the youth of this generation. Abba, we ask that they will declare it unashamedly, with power, unction and incredible boldness. Lord, we declare that man's opinions and political correctness will not silence their voice, in Jesus' name. We demand a seven fold return where the voice of the youth has been stolen, and we declare that they will proclaim the goodness of the Lord, and make straight a highway for the King to come!!! Thank You Jesus! Abba, let them know You!

(Jeremiah 20:9, Proverbs 6:31, Mark 1:3)

## ADOPTION

Abba, thank You that this is not an orphaned generation. You have called and chosen it. For our youth did not receive the spirit of slavery to fall back into fear, but You are calling them to receive the Spirit of adoption as Your children, by whom they can cry, "Abba! Father!" We ask that You would reveal Your incredible love to each one, that they would not fear anything but You. Let them know the joy and fullness of what it means to be a son and a daughter of the King! Thank You that because You live, the youth will live. Draw them, Jesus. Thank You that You will dwell in them and possess them and they will be one with You, Jesus. Let the fullness of Your love cast out any orphan spirit and let this generation know and live out of the fullness of who You have created them to be. Amen.

(John 14:16-20, Romans 8:15)

## FRUITFUL

Jesus, we thank You that You have created the youth to be like ones planted by streams of water. We declare that they will yield fruit in due season and whatever they do will prosper because they will be ones who meditate on Your word! Thank You for creating the youth, thank You that You knit each one together in their mother's womb and they are fearfully and wonderfully made! May their souls know this very well and give You glory, for the work that You have started in them that You will bring to completion! In Jesus' name, we say, "Come LORD Jesus come!"

(Psalm 1:1-3, Psalm 139:13-14, Philippians 1:6)

## FAITH

Thank You, Jesus, that You are raising up a
generation of great faith. Jesus, would You
increase faith in the youth even more, that they
may believe You, take You fully at Your word
and run with it. Thank You that they will be
ones of great faith, who through their actions will
demonstrate this, and will be ones who give You
no rest until You bring justice. Lord, You
promise that You will bring about justice quickly
for Your elect who cry out to You day and
night. Jesus, raise up youth in whom You can
find faith in on the earth. And fill them up with
Your love so that their faith; that is able to move
mountains, will not be in vain. Thank You
Jesus! We praise You for the good work that
You have started in each one. Amen.

(Luke 18:1-8, James 2)

# HUNGER & THIRST

Thank You Jesus for this generation that You are raising up to worship You in Spirit and in truth!  Thank You that You are seeking a people who will cry out louder than the rocks and seek Your face.  May the youth be a  bubbling brook overflowing with living waters.  Jesus, we pray that they would thirst for the water that satisfies.  We ask that You would even show them the right questions to ask, so that they could be satisfied with the water welling up to eternal life.  Thank You for an understanding of Your word, and that we can ask to know You!  Jesus, we ask that You would reveal Yourself to each youth, their families, and close friends.  May they know that they are loved, cared for and valued, in the Mighty name of Yeshua!  AMEN and AMEN!

(John 4:24, Luke 19:40, John 4:14)

## PREACHING

Father, we ask for a generation of youth that will
not be ashamed of the gospel of Christ, but that
they would be ones who believe the gospel  and
receive Your salvation!  Father, may these youth
hear the gospel, so that they could believe and be
completely set free, for who the Son sets free is
free indeed!  Raise them up to go in boldness
and be ones who will proclaim the gospel in
power with signs and wonders following,
bringing glory to You.  Father, we pray that this
would be a generation who will not care about
what others think of them.  May they be radical
lovers of the King; Powerhouses for your
name!!!

(John 8:36, Romans 1:16-17, Mark 16:20)

# TRANSFORMATION

Jesus, thank You so much for these leaders
rising up.  Thank You for the good work that
You have started in them, and for the seed that
has already been sown.  Father, we pray that the
seeds not be stolen from this generation.  Let
these youth be wise and observe what You have
done, so that they may understand Your loving-
kindness.  Father, we pray that they not just seek
after the signs and wonders, and the things You
can do, but let Your goodness wet their appetite
to search You out for who You are, out of a pure
heart.  Radically encounter this generation,
Abba; that in a moment they would be changed
forever because they have beheld the KING!
Even like Saul, Jesus, who wasn't even looking
for You, would You totally intercept the lives of
these youth and send them on a brand new
adventure that is beyond what they even dared to
dream!  Show them that You have a purpose for
their lives, and let them be fully wrecked for You
in an instant, in Jesus' name!

(Psalm 107:43, Mark 4:15, Acts 9:1:19)

## SALVATION

Jesus, we are asking for Your hand to be upon the youth. Abba, may they be ones who will lose their lives that they may gain them. Father, let them be ones who will hear the call and sell everything they have in order to gain You. Father, would You put a genuine cry in the hearts of these young men and women to ask You, "What must I do to be saved?" not like the rich ruler who asked You, but was unwilling to actually do what it took. But Jesus, may these youth cry out in truth in a pure heart, truly desiring to lay it all down to find You. Jesus, let them hear Your voice and do what You say, that they would not leave sorrowful because the cost is too great. May they find great joy in losing everything, but gaining You! Father, thank You that what is impossible with man is possible with You, so we ask that these youth would desire You enough to let You do the impossible in them. We decree salvation over this generation, in Jesus' name.

(Luke 17:33, Luke 18:18-27)

# LOVE

Father, we proclaim that this generation will know and encounter Your love! Father, draw their hearts to Yours. LORD, we pray that they would know that without love they really have obtained nothing. Father, we pray for pure eternal motives that are birthed from Your heart. We pray that these precious ones would encounter genuine love. Love is patient, and love is kind. It is not jealous, love does not brag and is not arrogant. It does not act unbecomingly and it does not seek its own. Love is not provoked, it does not take into account a wrong suffered, nor does it rejoice in unrighteousness, but rejoices with the truth. It bears all things, believes all things, hopes all things, and endures all things. Father we pray that like You, they would become love, in Jesus' name, amen.

(1 Corinthians 13:4-7)

# AWAKENING

Father, we are contending that this will be a
generation of holiness.  O God, would You
awaken the army of dry bones!  We ask that the
youth would be ones who are humble and
contrite before You.  Father, You are the High
and Holy One and You said You dwell in the
high and holy place with those who have a
contrite and humble spirit.  Lord, we're asking
that You would raise up ones who have the
honour of dwelling with You.  May they count
Your presence as worth more to them than
anything else.  You promised that You would
revive the spirit of the humble, and the heart of
the contrite ones, so would You revive the youth
right now!  We declare life over them!  We
declare an awakening to the calling of God.  We
decree over the youth, "Awake, you who sleep,
arise from the dead, and Christ will give you
light."  Father, we ask that they would be ones
whose greatest joy would be to imitate You.  We
decree that they are ones who will walk in love as
Christ has loved them and given Himself for
them!!!  We decree that uncleanness and filth
will have no part in their lives or speech, but that
they will walk in the holiness of Christ.  We
declare that they are ones who will listen only to
the truth of God.  We decree that though this
generation was once darkness that now they are
light in the Lord, and they will walk as children
of light!!!  We decree that they will search out
what brings You honour and joy and will walk in
the fruit of the Spirit, in righteousness and in

truth.  We declare that these are ones who will expose the works of darkness, and that all things exposed will be made manifest by the light. Father, we ask that You would raise up ones who would walk perfectly before You in all wisdom, redeeming the time.  We decree an understanding of the will of God, and a great thirst not for wine, but for the beauty of the Holy Spirit, constantly consumed by Him!!!  We decree over the youth an obsession with the King of kings!!!

(Isaiah 57:15,  Ephesians 5:1-18)

# HOLINESS

Jesus, thank You that You take great pleasure in this generation. Thank You that the youth are ones who will proclaim the truth without fear. Would You teach them the true gospel, so that the message in them would be like it was in Jeremiah, who said that even when he tried to contain it, Your word was like fire in his heart and shut up in his bones and he could not hold it in. Let Your word come alive in the young people! We call them forth to be ones through whom the kingdom of heaven can descend upon the earth. We declare that youth are an intersection between heaven and earth; that where they go, heaven comes. Awaken a hunger for You, Lord, and a discontent for the things of the world in the youth. Cause them to see the wicked, the vile and hate it; clinging to what is good. Let them plainly see the distinction between righteousness and wickedness. Protect their minds and hearts in Jesus' name. Thank You, Jesus, that You are able to keep them from stumbling and to present them faultless before the presence of Your glory with great joy. Mark this generation for Your kingdom, God, that no matter how hard the youth try to run from You, they cannot get away from Your presence.

(Jeremiah 20:9, Jude 1:24, Psalm 139:7-12,
Philippians 1:9-11)

# ENCOUNTER

Jesus, thank You for the youth! Thank You that
You are giving them a hunger and a thirst for
righteousness and that You are their answer.
You satisfy! Daddy, would You stir a
discontentment with status quo inside of them,
that normal would no longer be good enough for
any one of them, but that You would give these
ones a longing for You that drives them to seek
You relentlessly. Thank You for Your promise
that they will find You if they search for You
with all their hearts. Jesus, let the youth taste
and see that You are good, and let Your
kindness draw them to repentance. Radically
encounter this generation, Jesus, that even like
the disciples, that one encounter with the King
would be all it takes for them to leave everything
behind in pursuit of You. Let them meet You,
and never be the same again, in Jesus' name!

(Matthew 6:8, Jeremiah 29:13-14, Matthew 19:17)

# SONSHIP

Jesus, we thank You for youth and how You have made them.  Jesus, we thank You that You are so longing to pour out Your Spirit on the children; that You could declare over every one of them, "This is My Son in whom I am well pleased."  Jesus, You long for the day when these ones will run into Your arms and say, "Forgive me, for I did not know what I was doing.  I have longed to love You!"  Jesus, we declare that the youth will walk uprightly before You; pure and patient, holy and righteous!  Jesus, may the kingdom of heaven come upon them and their entire families!  Don't pass by this generation by without them encountering You and Your holiness!  The Spirit and the Bride say, "Come!"

(Luke 15:11-32,  Matthew 3:17, Exodus 33:17-19, Revelation 22:17)

# LEADERSHIP

Abba, thank You that You have marked this
generation for Your kingdom and for
leadership. Jesus, would You raise them up like
Elisha, who will pick up the mantle of those who
went before them and run with it. Even if they
can't see You, let them still move on, strike the
sea, and watch the waters part before them. Fill
them with a double portion of You, Holy Spirit,
that they can contain the fullness that You have
for them. Thank You that this generation is one
who will grab a hold of the promises of God and
not quit until they see the glory of God. Give
them great faith to believe You, Jesus, and to see
Your kingdom come on earth now. Thank You
that this generation is an overcoming generation.
Let them be ones who receive the full reward of
overcoming. Thank You Jesus, that through
You, they can run through a troop and leap over
a wall. In Jesus' name.

(2 Kings 2:8-14, Psalm 18:29)

## WARRIOR

Jesus, thank You that You have called the youth
out to be like Joshua, and lead a generation into
victory in You!  Father, we pray that they would
be strong and courageous, that they would not be
afraid or dismayed, for You are with them
wherever they go.  Daddy, would You give them
the revelation that Your love is their greatest
weapon, and that the weapons of their warfare
are not carnal, but mighty in You.  Let them be
strong in You, and in the power of Your might,
putting on the whole armor of God, so they can
stand against the wiles of the devil.  Jesus, would
You draw this generation!  Let them see that
You are worth giving up their lives for!  Let them
lose their lives, so they can actually find life in
You.  Teach them to follow You and imitate
You, so they can lead well, and raise a standard
for their generation!  Raise them up, Daddy!

(Joshua 1:9, 2 Corinthians 10:4, Ephesians 6:10-11,
Matthew 16:25)

# NEW CREATION

Thank You Father for the youth!!! Father, we are asking that You would raise them up to be like the Bereans, who heard the word, and then went and searched the scriptures for themselves to see if it was true. Father, would you give them a deep hunger to search into Your word. Father, remind them of what they have heard and seen You do, and let them wonder to the point of searching it out. Jesus, we ask that they would not forget, but that through searching You out for themselves, they would come to believe. Lord, we ask that this generation could get a hunger to search out Your word. Father, may they search for You, even if they come at night at first like Nicodemus, but let them not wait. We declare that these ones will not wait to seek for You until everyone else does, but that they will hunger for You enough that they will seek You themselves. Jesus, would You open their understanding to the mysteries of God. We declare that the youth will not be afraid to ask You the hard questions, but will ask, hear Your answer, and believe You. Burn in their hearts to talk with You constantly and to ask the things that are stirring and burning inside them. We declare that this next generation will not give in to fear, but will do whatever it takes to find You, In Jesus' name!

(Acts 17:11-12, John 3:1-21)

# FOLLOW

DAY 230

Jesus, thank You for the youth. Abba, we ask that even today You would rock them with Your presence. Holy Spirit would You descend on them like a dove even like You did on Jesus. Thank You that You have chosen them and called them Your beloved sons and daughters in whom You are well pleased. Jesus, let Your fire burn in them so that they are ready, not only to be imprisoned, but even to die for the name of the Jesus. Jesus, teach this generation to fix their eyes on You, not on the things on this earth. Jesus, we ask that every gain on earth would be like rubbish to them in comparison to knowing You and winning Christ. Let their goal be to be found in You, not having their own righteousness, which is of the law, but righteousness which is through Christ. Let them be faithful labourers and leaders for the glory of the King! Jesus, let them not be ones who look back, but sons and daughters who are fit for the kingdom of God. Jesus, we pray that the youth will be powerful, authoritative leaders not because of how well they lead, but by Your humility filling them. Jesus, let the same mind be in them that was in You. Let them be ones who will humble themselves to the point of laying down their lives for others just like You did. We speak freedom and purity and love over this generation, in Jesus' name.

(Acts 21:13, Acts 21:20, Philippians 3:9-10, Matthew 3:16-17, Colossians 3:2, Luke 10:2, Luke 9:62, Philippians 2:3-8)

# OVERCOMER

"Behold, I stand at the door and knock:. If any man hear my voice, and open the door, I will come in to him, and will dine with him, and he with me. To him who overcomes will I grant to sit with me in my throne, even as I also overcame, and am set down with my Father in his throne." Abba, thank You that You created this generation as overcomers. Open their ears to hear You. Fill them with the fear of the Lord which is the beginning of all wisdom and cause them to hate evil. Place Your fear in them, Abba, that will cause them to never leave You. Thank You for Your good promises towards the youth.

(Jeremiah 32:39-40, Revelation 3:20-21)

## SANCTIFICATION

Jesus, thank You for marking these young men
and women when they were little children.
Thank You for choosing each one of them from
before they were even born. Father, we ask that
these would be ones who know You like Moses
did. Jesus, we declare and call in that, like
Moses, the children in this generation will be
faithful in all Your house. Abba, let them know
You so well that You can speak with them face
to face, plainly, and that they can see the form of
the Lord. Daddy, You desire that they and their
whole families would be saved, so Jesus we ask
that the seed You planted in each one of them
would grow quickly to bear fruit and see their
whole families set on fire for You. These youth
are set apart ones, and we decree that today is
the day of salvation for them.

(Jeremiah 1:5, Numbers 12:7-8, 2 Corinthians 6:2)

# WISDOM

Jesus, thank You that Your truth sets us free. Holy Spirit, we ask that You would teach the children Your truth, for You are the One who guides us into all truth. Let them be filled with the fear of the Lord, which is the beginning of wisdom. Holy Spirit would You give them a revelation and understanding of the true gospel that sets men free, that You came to make all things new. We speak Your understanding over the youth, that they will have Your wisdom that is far more precious than gold. Thank You that You have given them great wisdom, discernment and great grace to act on it. We ask that Your grace that teaches us to say no to ungodliness and worldly passion would be multiplied toward each one in the knowledge of God and of Jesus our Lord. Jesus, we pray for these youth that their love might abound more and more in knowledge and in all judgment that they might approve things that are excellent. Jesus, we pray that they will be sincere and without offense until the day of Christ; being filled with the fruits of righteousness which are by Jesus Christ, for the glory and praise of God. Draw each one of them to Your heart that they can know You, the only true God and Jesus Christ whom You have sent.

(John 16:13, Proverbs 16:16, Titus 2:12, 2 Peter 1:2, Philippians 1:9-11, John 17:3)

## OVERCOMER

We thank You Jesus for these youth and for the amazing awesomeness that You have made each one to be, and that they will be ones to follow after You!  We thank You that no temptation has seized them except what is common to man.  And God, You are faithful!  You will not let the youth be tempted beyond what they can bear.  Rather, when they are tempted, You will provide a way out, so that they can stand up under it.  We ask that each one will be able to overcome and will be able to stand under the temptations that come their way.  We thank You that You will show the youth the more excellent way!

(1 Corinthians 10:13, 1 Corinthians 12:31)

# SEARCHING

Jesus, we ask that the youth would come to You,
the Fountain of Living Waters. May they
recognize You and ask You for the living water,
to never ever thirst again!!! Father, may they
drink of You, that they would never thirst, and
the water would become in them a fountain of
water springing up into everlasting life! Father,
we ask that these youth would taste and see that
You are good. That in all their searching, they
would taste You, and discover that You are what
they have been searching for all along! Jesus, we
ask that none of them would be afraid of what
their friends or family will say or do, but that
their hunger for You would drive them to search
You out anyway. Father, would You help them
to find You before it's too late. Father, would
the emptiness drive the youth to seek You and
not to give up. We declare life, and life
abundantly over this generation, in Jesus'
name!!

(Jeremiah 2:13, Psalm 34:8, John 4:10-14, John 10:10)

# IDENTITY

Abba, we thank You for the promise that You
have not forgotten the younger generation, but
You know each one of them.  You know
everything about them.  You know when they sit
and when they rise, You are familiar with all
their ways and You know their thoughts before
they think them.  You knit them together in their
mother's womb.  Before they were even born
You knew them and chose them.  Abba, You
have not forgotten them, because You have
engraved them on the palms of Your hands.
Thank You, Jesus, that You say to the youth,
"Before I formed you in the womb I knew you,
and before you were born I consecrated you; I
appointed you a prophet to the nations."  Thank
You, Jesus, that they are fearfully and
wonderfully made.  We ask that You would
secure in their hearts the truth of their identity in
You.  Abba, thank You that these ones were not
hidden from You when You formed them in
secret.  Every day of their lives You wrote in
Your book even before they took one breath.
Your thoughts toward the youth are as many as
the sands of the sea.  Jesus, would You
overwhelm each one of them with Your love
right now and let them hear a few of Your
amazing thoughts towards them.  Let them walk
in the boldness  and the fullness of who You say
that they are.  Open their ears to hear the songs
that You are singing over them.

(Psalm 139:1-6, Isaiah 49:15-16, Psalm 139:13-18,
Zephaniah 3:17, Jeremiah 1:5)

DAY 236

# PERSECUTION

Thank You, Jesus, that You knew this
generation that would follow You before the
foundations of the earth and You say it is
good!  Jesus, we pray that these youth would
begin to get a firm foundation; that they would
begin to hunger and thirst for righteousness.
Would You begin to birth a desire in their hearts
to know You, to know nothing but the cross and
Christ crucified!  We pray that in this season
youth all over the world would pray for their
enemies and bless those who persecute them,
knowing that it may be what is needed to save
their enemies.  Please give them the strength to
fight for what's worth fighting for, and let go of
what's not!  Amen!!!

(Ephesians 4:31-32, Ephesians 1:4, Romans 8:29,
Jeremiah 1:5a, Ephesians 1:11, Genesis 1:31,
1 Corinthians 1:25, Acts 7:60, John 15:20)

DAY 237

## IDENTITY

Jesus, thank You that You have called these children Your own, and that they are Your jewel. They are Your greatest treasure, and the delight of Your heart. Abba, would You give them a revelation of their identity in You, and that they are beautiful just the way You made them because they were made in Your image. Give them eyes to see the way You see. Father, may the youth be ones who see things for what they are and call it out; that they will be ones with eyes open to discern between the righteous and the wicked, and not whitewash the things that grieve Your heart. Give them a hunger and thirst for righteousness, Abba. As they seek first Your kingdom and Your righteousness, let everything these youth have need of be added to them. O' Jesus, let them become so enraptured by You that the opposite kingdom suddenly becomes repulsive, in Jesus' name.

(Malachi 3:17-18, Psalm 149:4)

# LOVE

Daddy, would You raise up young men and
women as ones who know You. Abba, let them
be ones who are so filled with Your love and
Your heart that they can go into the darkest
places full of love, always believing, hoping and
enduring, pressing in for Your heart to be
fulfilled. Raise them up O God! Would You
show these ones what it looks like to really love
You and be Yours! Thank You that the youth
are patient, the youth are kind, the youth are not
jealous or boastful, the youth are not arrogant or
rude. Thank You that the youth do not rejoice
in wrong, but rejoice in the truth. Abba, would
You so save each one of them and set them on
fire that they could know Your path, and the
fullness of joy, even in persecution, that comes
from being in Your presence. Daddy, let all who
see these ones bring You glory! Thank You that
the youth are the fragrance of Christ, first to
You, then to the world!!!

(1 Corinthians 13:4-7, Psalm 16:11)

# GOD'S POSSESSION

DAY 240

Abba, thank You for the young ones. Thank You for their persistence in calling forth the things that are not as though they were, and believing against all odds that You are able to do what You have promised. Jesus draw each one to Your heart that they would know You. Let this generation be filled with all the fullness of God. We call out Your dream over each one of their lives, that they will be one with You. Abba, let these be ones who are watching, waiting and ready at the coming of Jesus. Let them be ones upon whom You will gaze and say, "I know her. I know him. They are mine". Finish the good work that You have started in each one individually and in this generation as a whole. Let these youth be desperately hungry for You.

(Romans 4:17, Philippians. 1:6)

# BOLDNESS

Thank You Jesus, for the youth. Thank You for Your compassion for them. O Righteous Father, even though the world does not know You, may this generation know You, and may those around them know that You have sent them. Would You give the youth the boldness to make Your name known, and the drive to continue to make it known, that the love with which You have loved them would also be in each one of their classmates! Jesus, Your word says that the righteous are as bold as a lion, so let Your righteousness rise up in this generation. Give the youth the grace to be able to do the things You are calling them to, so they may see Your Kingdom come in their schools as it is in heaven! Thank You, Jesus, that You are righteous and You have shown us how to walk. We ask that You give this generation the strength to become as You were so that others may live, in Jesus' name.

(John 17:25-26, Proverbs 28:1)

# LEADERSHIP

DAY 242

Abba, thank You for the treasure that You have created each youth to be. They are Your treasure hidden in the field that You gave Your life to seek out and find and possess. We ask, God, that You would give them a willingness to surrender and lose their lives for Your sake, so that they can find their lives in You. Let this generation not be intimidated or afraid to lose control and give it to You. We ask that any need the youth would feel for control because of wounding would go in Jesus' name, and that each one would be able to rest and be all the fullness of the men and women of God that You created them to be. Let them rise up. Many are leaders with huge influence, so train them how to lead well. Thank You that they will set an example for the believers in speech, in life, in love, in faith and in purity. Abba, let these ones be like David who, even as a young man, was willing to fight the giant when not even the trained soldiers were willing. Enable them to rise up and fight. We proclaim they will defeat that giant for the glory of Your name, and all people will know through their lives that You are God! Praise the Lord!

(Matthew 13:44, Matthew 16:33, 1 Timothy 4:12)

# SEARCHING

Jesus, thank You that this is the generation that
will prepare a way for You.  That the youth of
our generation are the voice of one crying in the
wilderness, "Prepare the way of the LORD;
Make straight in the desert a highway for our
God."  Thank You for the call of righteousness
and holiness that You have on each one of their
lives.  Abba, we ask that You draw them deep,
deep into Your heart in this season, and teach
them how to steward that well.  Jesus, would
You take each one to that place where they
know You so well that they start to naturally live
to  the sound of Your heartbeat.  Give them eyes
to see the way that You see, Jesus.  Let them
know You!  Father, we pray that You take these
youth into a season of cultivating an intimacy
with You that they have never had before.  Let
them hunger and thirst so deeply for
righteousness that they may be satisfied.  Abba,
we ask that this would be a generation with a
Psalm 119 hunger for You and for Your word,
and an insatiable thirst for You that will cause
them to seek after You with their whole hearts.
Open their eyes to see wondrous things from
Your law, and let it become their delight.

(Isaiah 40:3, Matthew 5:6, Psalm 119:18, Psalm 119:174)

DAY 243

## ARISE

Abba, let this generation cry out to You from the depths of their souls! Father, raise up these young men and women as a trumpet in this last hour to call forth Your people into victory. Use their justice and strong sense of right and wrong to keep them tightly knit to You on the straight and narrow path that You have laid out for them. May Your word be a lamp to their feet and a light to their path!

(Psalm 130:1, Matthew 7:14, Psalm 119:105)

# BOLD PROCLAMATION

Abba, thank You that You have chosen the youth to carry the good news. Thank You that their feet are shod with the readiness of the gospel of peace. Thank You that they are ones who will understand the message and proclaim it boldly to all nations, tongues, tribes and people. Thank You that this is the generation who will truly fulfill the great commission; they will go into all the world and proclaim the gospel to every creature, teaching them to obey everything that You have commanded, baptizing them in the name of the Father, Son and Holy Spirit, and signs and wonders will follow, confirming the message. Abba, let the gospel become more than just words to them, let it come alive inside of them; that the fullness of the life You have planned for each one would come to pass. Abba, we thank You that even if tribulation, or distress, or persecution, or famine, or nakedness, or peril, or sword tries to separate them from Your love; if they are for Your sake counted as a sheep for the slaughter, that even in all these things these youth are more than conquerors through Jesus who loves them. Abba, let them be persuaded that neither death, nor life, nor angels, nor principalities, nor powers, nor things present nor things to come, nor height, nor depth, nor any other created thing, shall be able to separate them from the love of God which is in Christ Jesus our Lord.

(Ephesians 6, Matthew 28:18-20, Mark 16:15-18, Mark 16:20, 1 Timothy 4:12, Romans 8:36-39, John 14:30)

DAY 245

# SENT

Abba, we're asking that You would raise up this generation as end time warriors who will call in the return of Christ. We decree that these youth are young men and women who will prophesy and receive the Holy Spirit, that they are ones who will call on the name of the Lord and be saved. Father, You promised that in the last days You would pour out Your Spirit on all flesh, and our sons and daughters would prophesy, young men will see visions and old men will dream dreams. Father, we believe You and we are pressing in for that for the youth! May they be ones who give You their complete yes and are ekballoed into Your kingdom and mission! Father, we decree that these are the ones who will behold You always before their face, that because You are at their right hand they will not be shaken. We declare that their hearts will rejoice and their tongues be glad, their flesh also will rest in hope. Father, we ask that these youth would know the ways of life and find great fullness of joy in Your presence!!! Abba, may they seek after You and fix their gaze upon You, finding their meaning, purpose and fulfillment completely in You and Your presence!!! LORD keep their hearts soft in this last hour. Help them to humble themselves before You, and cast ALL their cares upon You.

(1 Peter 5:7; Revelation 12:11, Matthew 24:12, Acts 2:17-28)

# PERSEVERANCE

LORD, we thank You for the youth of our generation. We pray that Your relationship with each one would come to new heights. You know their deeds and their toil and perseverance. We decree that these are ones who will not tolerate that which is evil and that they will put to the test those who call themselves apostles but are not, and that they will find them to be false. Father, we thank You that You have given each one the ability to persevere and endure for Your name's sake, and we decree that these are ones who will not grow weary. LORD, may You always be their first love and let them never forget You or put You second in their lives. May they always remember the heights You have placed them on and let repentance be quick at hand for them. Father, we pray that these young men and women would have full knowledge of what happens if they walk away from You, so that they will stay on the straight and narrow path. We pray that each one will always hate what You hate and love what You love. Father, we ask that You give them ears to hear, eyes to see, a mind to perceive and a heart that can receive all that You say and do. Father, we thank You that their reward for overcoming is that they will eat from the tree of life in the paradise of God!

(Revelations 2:1-7)

# WARRIOR

Jesus, thank You that You have called the youth
to be soldiers in Your army. May it be to them
according to Your word, "Be strengthened by
the grace that is in Christ Jesus, and what you
have heard from me in the presence of many
witnesses, entrust to faithful men who will be
able to teach others also. Share in suffering as a
good soldier of Christ Jesus. No soldier gets
entangled in civilian pursuits, since his aim is to
please the one who enlisted him." Thank You
that these are ones who will have the grace to say
no to participating in the things of this world, so
that they will please You. We ask, Jesus, that
You would give them great understanding in the
gospel, that they would be like the hardworking
farmer who has the first share of the crops, and
we ask that it be a full share. Raise them up like
Josiah, O God, who tore down all the altars of
Baal and not like Jehu who destroyed all the
descendants of Ahab's house, but he did not
follow You with all His heart. Abba, let it be
said of the youth that they are ones who have
turned to You with all their heart, all their soul,
and all their might. Let this generation be the
one, Abba. Let them be the Gideon warriors
whom You called forth and You empowered.
May they obey You against all odds. Train their
hands for war and their fingers to fight. Equip
them to overcome the enemy through worship,
praise, dance and prayer. Thank You Jesus!

(2 Timothy 2:1-7, 2 Kings 10:31, 2 Kings 23:25,
Psalm 144:1)

DAY 248

# FEARLESS

Jesus, thank You for the strength and boldness that You have given the youth. Thank You that You have called them out to run with You. Jesus, thank You that You have commanded them to be strong and of good courage, to not be afraid or dismayed because You are with them wherever they go. Jesus, thank You that the youth will be Joshuas or Calebs for this generation; that they will see Your promise and stand on it and will not bow to the majority that says it can't be done! Thank You that these chosen ones will not be swayed by the 'yes, buts,' but that they will fearlessly take the land that You have given them, because You are with them. Jesus, give the youth the tenacity to believe You for the impossible! Let the fear of man have absolutely no hold on them, but let them fear You and only You! Thank You, Jesus! You are so good!

(Joshua 1:9, Numbers 13:30-33, Numbers 14:1-9)

## BOLDNESS

Jesus, thank You for the children. Abba, would You raise them up strong and courageous. You said that the righteous are bold as a lion. May they be clothed in Your righteousness! Jesus, we pray that in any areas where they have called themselves insignificant that You would reveal Your truth to them. Jesus, nothing Goliath said could terrify David because he knew who You were. So Jesus, we ask that You would raise the youth up as strong warriors, not in themselves, but in knowing that they can do nothing of themselves, but in You each one of them is powerfully equipped. Father, give these ones the boldness to just try it and to find that when they are weak then they are strong. We declare that fear of man has no hold on them, but that this generation will choose the favor of God, rather than the favor of man. Jesus, we're asking that, like David, You would put Your cause in the hearts of the youth, that they would be willing to step out and fight to see Your cause fulfilled through them. We declare a clear call and a clear cause over this generation right now, in Jesus' name.

(1 Samuel 17, 2 Corinthians 12:9-10)

# STRENGTH

LORD, You have created the youth to be strong
fighters! So we declare over them, "Be Strong!
Fight bravely for the people and the cities that
God is giving you. Know that God will do
through you what is good in His sight if you will
give Him your YES!" God has girded this
generation with strength for battle and will
subdue their enemies.

(Psalm 18:39, 2 Samuel 10:12)

# LOVE

Abba, we thank You for the young people.
Thank You that they will truly be ones to lay
down their lives, so that others can live.  Thank
You for the love and compassion that You are
birthing in them, that just like Jesus each one of
them will be moved with compassion for those
around them and be filled with Your love that
compels them to action.  Thank You, Jesus, that
Your love is their greatest weapon, so we ask
that You train their hands for war, and their
fingers for battle, but that their battles would be
won with love because You are love.  Fill this
generation with a love that is so crazy that
nothing can stand in their way because they
know exactly who they are and who You are.
Father, we're asking for such a childlike faith for
these youth, that they will run with You to the
craziest of places simply because they trust You
and obey You.  Thank You that these will be
ones who will follow You even if it makes no
logical sense and in so doing will completely
confound the minds of the wise.  In Jesus'
name!  Amen.

(Matthew 9:36, John 15:13, Psalm 144:1,
1 Corinthians 1:27)

# HOLINESS

Daddy, would You raise up this generation to
know the holiness of God. Father, we are asking
that the youth would dwell in high and holy
places with You. Father, would You create in
them a contrite and humble spirit, so that they
can dwell with You. Father, we ask that these
would be ones who walk uprightly and work
righteousness, ones who speak truth in their
hearts. Father, we ask that they would be ones
who do not backbite with their tongues, nor do
any evil to their neighbours, nor take up a
reproach against their friends. Father, may they
not despise a vile person, but honour those who
fear the Lord. May this generation not turn
away from You, Abba, even if they swear to their
own hurt; may they not put out their money as a
usury, nor take a bribe against the innocent.
Father, You promised that those who do these
things will never be moved and You said that
these are the ones who may abide in Your
tabernacle and dwell in Your holy hill. Abba, we
ask that You would raise up a generation to
know the truth and holiness of You, and to walk
in it, completely unashamed. We declare that
the youth are ones who will not be moved, in
Jesus' name.

(Isaiah 57:15, Psalm 15)

# FEAR OF THE LORD

Abba, thank You that You have appointed this generation for greatness. Thank You that You are calling the youth as ones who will stand before governors and kings on Your account as witnesses to them. We ask, God, that You would teach them wisdom and the fear of the Lord. The fear of the Lord is to hate evil, so let the fear of God be so rooted in the youth that nothing of this world will be able to draw them away from You. Holy Spirit all the words of Your mouth are righteous, and wickedness is an abomination to Your lips, so we ask that You would so fill the youth that wickedness would be an abomination to their lips, just like it is to Yours. Let nothing defiling come out of their mouths. From the overflow of the mouth the heart speaks, so let wickedness be an abomination to their hearts and whole beings, and let them delight in the fear of the Lord. Teach these ones to love You, Father, with ALL their hearts, with ALL their souls and with ALL their strength and with ALL their minds. Fill the children with Your wisdom now, so that they can be the leaders You have made them to be. Let them fear You above all else and be drawn to Your liquid love. Thank You that they will walk in holiness and righteousness before You.

(Matthew 10:18, Proverbs 8:13, Matthew 22:37-39, Proverbs 8:15-16, Philippians 1:9-11)

# ENCOUNTER

Thank You Abba, for the youth. Thank You that You have qualified them to be partakers of the inheritance of the saints. Jesus, would You show them that You have incredible plans for each one of them, and that they can be used by You! Daddy would You give these chosen ones radical faith in You! That they would dare to believe You for the impossible, and watch You do the greater works because they believed You! Let them see You, and know You so well that the counterfeits no longer have a hold on them because they have been captivated by You. Father we pray that the youth be ones who's longing for You is so pure that You come; that they would be ones to take the seventy up onto the mountain to meet with You, and literally behold You, simply because they loved You so well. Do it God! Draw each one, and let them be permanently wrecked for You, that nothing be able to sway them to the right or to the left anymore, because they have beheld the KING!

(Colossians 1:12, John 14:12, Exodus 24:9-11)

## PERSEVERANCE

God You are soooo good and sooooo glorious. Your love towards the youth is soooo rich! We pray that they will know the heights and depths of Your love for them. We pray that they would be able to persevere under pressure & trial knowing that having stood the test, they will receive the crown of LIFE that You promised to those who love You. Father we pray that You would deposit a rich love for You inside of this generation that would continue to grow daily. LORD we ask that You cause a stirring for Your word to penetrate each youth and stir them to hunger and thirst for righteousness. We pray that there would be a deep and rich desire to know You and to seek You out. Good and glorious Father, we ask that these youth would have powerful encounters with You that would radically shape and shift them into the plans and purposes of God!

(James 1:12, Ephesians 3:18)

# LOVE

Thank You for how amazingly You created this generation. Abba, would You place Your Spirit on each child that they would be Your chosen servants, Your beloved ones with whom Your soul is well pleased. We pray they will proclaim justice to the nations victoriously through Your name and Your blood shed on the cross. Jesus, thank You that this generation is one that will carry Your authority well in love. God would You grow Your love that is patient and kind, not jealous or boastful, not arrogant or rude in each youth; Your love that does not insist on its own way, it is not irritable or resentful; Your love that does not rejoice in iniquity, but rejoices in the truth; Your love that bears all things, believes all things, hopes all things and endures all things; Your love that never fails. Let the youth be ones who will do everything out of love for You first and then for the people. Thank You Jesus, that they will grow in godly authority because it comes from a place of love. Thank You that the children are a weapon in Your hand and they will crush the head of the enemy. Let their first weapon be love, in Jesus' name. Let Your love that abhors evil and clings to what is good fill this generation, in Jesus' name, that they would love their enemies and the least of these and that You would confirm the power of Your love, even through Your signs and wonders following them.

(Matthew 12:18-21, 1 Corinthians 13:1-8, Genesis 3:15, Romans 12:9-21, Mark 16:20

# FRAGRANCE

Abba, thank You for the youth and the brilliant minds that You have given them. Abba, let this generation be like Job; ones who are perfect and upright before You and who fear You and shun evil. Thank You that You are so proud of them and we ask, would You enable them by Your grace to pass the test like Job did, so that no matter what comes against them, that their hearts would not grow cold and that they would not curse You, falsely accuse, or sin in any way. Let this generation be the one that falls at Your feet and worships You and blesses Your name in every situation. Thank You that the youth are overcomers. Thank You that You lead them in triumph in Christ, and through them defuse the fragrance of Christ's knowledge in every place. Thank You Jesus, that before anything else, this generation is a sweet smelling fragrance to You and You are so pleased with them, Abba. Thank You that You are good and the youth are the abode of the Good, so You abide with and within them. We call them into the destiny You have for this generation. Thank You for the wisdom that You have given them that will even confound the minds of those who are wise on earth and will teach them the fear of the Lord. Let their boast forever be in the Lord.

(Job 1:1, Job 1:8, Job 1:22, 2 Corinthians 2:14-15, 1 Timothy 4:12, Proverbs 2, 1 Corinthians 1:27)

# FOLLOW

Jesus, let this generation be the ones who forsake all and follow You! Father, let them not just be astonished by what You do, but by who You are. Jesus, would You draw them into the prayer closet to be with You, to desire You and to encounter You in the secret place. Jesus, just as the secret place with the Father was Your favorite place to be, let the same be true for the youth, that no matter the crazy places You take them, they will always stay rooted in You and in prayer. Jesus, let the youth be ones who follow hard after You! Give them the tenacity to seek You until they find You! Daddy, let them never give up! Put such a burning desire in this generation to seek and keep seeking, to knock and keep knocking and to ask and keep asking because You are a Father who loves to give good gifts to His kids. Thank You for encountering the youth even today, so that they will be rocked by You and will give their lives to follow after You. May they count everything else as worthless compared to the prize of knowing You!

(Luke 5:16, Psalm 63:8, Jeremiah 29:12-13, Matthew 7:7-8, Luke 5:11, Luke 5:9-10, Philippians 3:8)

## CAPTIVATED

Father, we ask that You open the youth's eyes to see You; that they would receive such a revelation of You, and behold You in such a way that everything else completely fades away. Let them be captivated by Your beauty, by Your holiness, by Your love! Abba, let this generation truly be one whose gaze is forever fixed on You. Let them love You well! Let them love You with ALL their heart, ALL their soul, ALL their mind and ALL their strength. May the youth be ones who will give You their all- completely sold out lovers of the KING! Let them go quickly and sell all that they have to gain You, never to look back again. Jesus, would You have your way with this generation!

(Luke 10:27, Matthew 13:44)

# IDENTITY

Thank You, Abba, that the youth are jewels and treasures in Your hand. You hold them in the palm of Your hand and You will not forget anyone of them for You have engraved them on the palm of Your hand. Thank You for creating this generation to be a crown of beauty- a royal diadem- in Your hand LORD. Who are You, O God, to show forth Your power and love through the youth! Thank You, Jesus, that You call the children to come and sit with You under the apple tree and enjoy You and be loved by You. Would You show Yourself strong on their behalf, O God. They are like Davids, who although they looked to be the least, You chose them to be kings of the nation and when everyone else is too afraid, the youth will slay the giant!

(Isaiah 49:16, Isaiah 62:3, Song of Songs 2:3, Psalm 68:28)

# FAITHFULNESS

Thank You Jesus that the youth are super precious to You. Jesus, You say, "Let the little children come to Me and do not hinder them, for to such belongs the kingdom of Heaven." Thank You, Jesus. Let the children be like the wise steward who was faithful with what You entrusted him with and multiplied it for Your kingdom and Your glory. Let them be like the boy with five loaves and two fish, who brought what he had and laid it all at Your feet. Multiply it in the lives of the youth, so that multitudes will be fed of You. Thank You Jesus that the children are the catalyst for a miracle and a move of God. They will surrender their part to You and have the faith of a child to let You do the rest. Let the youth be the ones who will stand before You, and hear You say, "Well done good and faithful servant." Let them be faithful with the little, so that You can entrust them with much. Let them enter into the joy of their Lord.

(Luke 18:16, Matthew 19:14, John 6:9,
Matthew 25:20-24)

# WORSHIP

Father, let the children be ones who will worship
You in Spirit and in truth, the way You long to
be worshipped.  Let the cry of their hearts simply
be to touch the heart of the King.  Father, we
pray that these be ones who will say to You,
"Your face, Lord, I will seek!"  Abba, let each
one of the youth catch one true glimpse of the
King that changes everything.  Let them be so
enraptured by Your beauty, that You are the one
thing that they desire.

(Psalm 27:4)

## DEVOTION

Jesus, thank You for who You have made the youth to be. Father, we ask that as You call them to follow You and be Your disciples, that they would hear You and follow You all the way without conditions or excuses. We decree that this generation is one who will love You enough that they will follow You, even if it means they have nowhere to lay their heads. Jesus, we ask that You would burn in them and give the youth the grace to love You more than they love even their own family; that their loyalty to You would be first. We decree that the youth will see that there is no one like God and will pour out their very lives at Your feet. We decree that the lives of the youth will be worship poured out on Your feet, filling the whole nation with the fragrance of lives laid down with a burning love for Jesus! Thank You that this generation brings You great joy!!!

(Matthew 8:18-20, Luke 18:29-30, John 12:3)

# BLESSING

Father, we thank You that as the children
faithfully obey You and are careful to follow
You all the days of their lives, that You will bring
them into the greatness of God. LORD, let
Your goodness and blessings overtake this
generation! May the youth be blessed at home
and at school; bless their families' income
revenue streams, bless the relationships in their
family, bless their talents and hobbies as
well. LORD, bless the youth when they come in
and when they go out. Father, we thank You
that all the youth need to do is love all those who
mistreat them and it is Your responsibility to
deal with anyone who would bother or harass
them on account of loving You. Father, we pray
that this generation will hear Your heartbeat
when You say, "Love your enemies, do good to
those who hate you, bless those who curse you,
pray for those who mistreat you. If someone
strikes you on one cheek, turn to him the other
also." We ask that they would love their
enemies and pray for those who mistreat them,
so that they would be called children of God
Most High. You, O God, You cause the sun to
rise on the good and evil and send rain on the
righteous and wicked because Your love for us is
not based on what we do, but who You are.

(Luke 6:27-29, Matthew 5:43-45, Deuteronomy 28:1-6)

## COURAGE

Jesus, we just pray for young leaders right now
that they would be strong and courageous, not
terrified or dismayed for You, Lord God, are
with them wherever they go. Thank You for the
incredible, nation-shifting, out-of-the-box
courage that You have placed in the youth. We
call it out right now, in Jesus' name, and release
them to walk in the fullness of their destiny. Let
them not be discouraged, terrified or dismayed.
Would You give them understanding of Your
perfect love that casts out all fear. Abba, thank
You that the youth are ones who will not be
ashamed or shrink back at Your coming, but
they will be ones who abide in You. Holy Spirit,
would You show them how to walk out Your
powerful gospel, that whoever abides in You
ought to walk as You walked, and that You fully
forgive and cleanse them from all sin, so that the
enemy will have nothing in them. You are the
Savior of the world, Jesus! Thank You for Your
love for the children. Give them understanding
to know how wide, deep, long and high Your
love is.

(1 John 2:28, Ephesians 3:18, 1 John 2:6, Joshua 1:9)

# THIRST

Jesus, thank You that You promised that whoever is thirsty can come to You and drink. Abba, we ask that You would draw the children to You right now. Jesus, would You tenderize their hearts towards You, so they can know You! Let them taste and see that You really are good! Thank You that when the youth drink of the water that You will give them, they will never thirst, but the water that You give these ones will become in them a fountain of water springing up into everlasting life. Abba, give them the courage to take a drink of You. Show them Your heart. Abba, let them taste of You and never be the same again! Thank You for their salvation. We declare their mourning is turning to dancing, in Jesus' name!!!

(John 4:14, Psalm 30:11)

# TREASURED

Abba, thank You for the youth. Thank You so much for how precious You see them. Thank You that they are a crown of splendor in Your hand and a royal diadem in the hand of their God. Abba, would You reveal to them how precious their lives are in Your sight, that they are engraved in the palm of Your hand and You will never forget them. We command all lies of the enemy speaking to youth to go right now. Let them hear the voice of the King loudly and clearly. Abba, set them free to live out of Your love. Thank You that it is for freedom that You are setting the youth free. They are Your treasured ones. Reveal to each one that they are Your pearl of great price and Your treasure that You gave everything for. Abba, fill them with Your love. We speak the Father's love over each one. Thank You that the youth are accepted in the Beloved and they no longer have to struggle to find acceptance because they have found it in You. We call forth this generation as one who will speak Your life into people and MANY will find You through them. Thank You Jesus that these ones will know that they are children of the King and that You are their Abba, Father. Let their spirits cry out, "Abba, Father!" Encourage the youth in You today and send Barnabases to encourage the youth to be all that You created them to be.

(Isaiah 62:3, Isaiah 49:16, Galatians 5:1, Song of Songs 6:3, Matthew 13:44-46, Ephesians 1:6, Romans 8:15)

# IDENTITY

Jesus thank You for the young people!  Abba,
You have made each one fearfully and
wonderfully!  They are Your own treasured
possession!  Daddy, would You give them such a
revelation of their identity in You of Your heart
toward them.  Jesus, would You let them see a
glimpse of what they look like to You, and how
You see them.  Give the youth Your eyes to see
the beauty of what You have made.  Father, let
them be so settled in what You say about them
that what others say about them would not
matter; that these would never need to seek
approval from people because You are their
approval, and You have accepted them, chosen
them, predestined them to adoption as Your
sons and daughters, according to the good
pleasure of Your will.  Thank You that the youth
will be ones to call out the gold in others because
You have called out the gold in each of them.
Abba, let them taste and see Your goodness, and
be undone by the extravagance of Your love for
them, in Jesus' name.

(Psalm 139:14, Deuteronomy 7:6, Ephesians 1:3-6,
Psalm 34:8)

# HOLINESS

Father, would You raise this generation up to be ones who embraces Your holiness. Abba, let the youth see the truth of who You are and run with it. Jesus, we ask that they would see the truth of the gospel and not be ashamed of it, but would be ones who powerfully proclaim the gospel, resulting in salvation for everyone who believes. Father, we are asking that the youth would have the revelation that You are light and there is no darkness at all in You, and if we claim to be in You there can't be any darkness in us either. Daddy, raise them up to run powerfully with the gospel. Raise them up O God! Set them free! Let them know You! We decree a radical transformation and salvation for the children and youth, that they will be ones who are completely dead in the flesh, that Christ may live in them. We decree that they are ones who will abide in Jesus and not practice sin and will be unashamed of the holiness You have called them to walk in, in Jesus' name!

(Romans 1:16, 1 John 1:5, Galatians 2:20, 1 John 3:6)

# BOLDNESS

Abba, thank You for the incredible boldness that You have given the youth. Thank You that You have made them fearless warriors for the kingdom. Jesus, would You let them see it! Let the youth see themselves the way that You see them. Give this generation a revelation of who they are in You. Jesus, would You even show them that with You all things are possible, even the dreams that they have hidden in the deepest part of their hearts because You were the One who gave them those dreams, so it's okay to dream big! Thank You that the youth don't have to wait till they are grown up for You to use them, but like Samuel and Josiah they have a voice -now- and You can and will use them powerfully! Thank You that You have not given them a spirit of fear, but of power, and of love, and of a sound mind. Thank You Jesus, that the youth are example setters and bar raisers, in Jesus' name!

(Psalm 37:4, 2 Timothy 1:7, 1 Timothy 4:12)

## LOVE

Jesus, thank You for the youth of this generation. Thank You that they are called by You. Father, we ask that You would draw them close to Your heart. Thank You that You gather them in Your arms. Jesus, we ask that the youth would be ones who radically follow and love You and that they will love and bless even those who hate them and mistreat them. Teach the youth how to give abundantly, even when stolen from; that they will give to everyone who asks of them and that just as they desire others to do to them, they will do to others as well. Thank You that the youth are ones who will love radically and without measure, hoping for nothing in return. Thank You that they are the ones who will carry Your heart and Your character so well that multitudes will encounter You. Jesus, thank You that this generation is one that is merciful, just as You also are merciful. We declare radical encounters with You over the youth that will leave them totally undone for anything less than the fullness of God manifest in them!

(Isaiah 40:11, Luke 6:27-36)

# INTIMACY

Jesus, we ask right now that You would heal the hearts of the youth by Your blood.  Thank You Jesus that the youth are ones who are filled with compassion and love and who will behold the Lord like Moses did and who will know God face to face.  Jesus, let the children enter into a place of intimacy with You right now, not just when they are older.  Thank You for how You have encountered them.  Jesus, let the youth be ones who will walk in humility like You did, Jesus, who will kneel down and wash the feet of their betrayers.  Let them humble themselves and become servants like You did Jesus, that the same mind would be in them that was also in Christ Jesus.  You humbled Yourself and became obedient to death on the cross.  Jesus, we thank You that Your radical love will overflow in the youth, so that no matter who or what hurts them or speaks against them, all that flows out of the youth will be love and that their automatic response will be to forgive and love them.  Let them be wrecked for Your presence.  We ask, Jesus, that the youth will literally see You face to face and be undone by You.  You say to this generation, "I will do this thing, also, that you have spoken, for you have found grace in My sight and I know you by name.  I will make My goodness pass before you."

(Deuteronomy 34:10, John 13:2-5, Philippians 2:5-8, Exodus 33:15, Exodus 33:17-19, Matthew 17:20)

## COURAGE

Thank You, Abba, for the boldness that You
have given the youth.  Thank You that they will
be strong and courageous, that they will not be
afraid or dismayed because You are with them
wherever they go.  Give this generation a
revelation of their identity in You, Jesus, so that
they will be unshakable and untouchable because
they know who they are, and they know Who
You are.  Thank You Jesus, that the youth will
route entire armies simply by worshipping and
praising You!  Let them stand still and see the
salvation of the LORD.  Jesus, You are good
and Your mercies endure forever!

(Joshua 1:9, 2 Chronicles 20:22, Exodus 14:13)

# FORGIVEN

Abba, we thank You for this generation!!!
Father, we ask that they would be ones who
would know You; that the love with which You
have loved Jesus may be in them and that You,
Jesus, may be in them.  Father, we ask that the
youth know how much You have done for them;
the richness of Your forgiveness and the power
of the cross.  Father, we ask that as the youth
see what You have done for them that they
would not only receive Your forgiveness, but
that it would compel them to overlook offenses
as well.  We declare that this generation is one
who will forgive even seventy times seven, and
will have compassion on others, just as You have
had compassion on them.

(Matthew 18:21-35, John 17:26, 1 Peter 4:8)

## PRAISE

Thank You Jesus for the youth. Thank You for
Your love. Thank You that You are drawing
them to Your heart in this season. Thank You
that You take their mourning and turn it into
dancing. You take their sorrow and turn it into
JOY!!! You have taken off the youth's sackcloth
and clothed them with joy, that their soul may
sing praises to You and not be silent. O Lord
God, we declare the youth will give thanks to
You forever. Continue to draw them and woo
them, Lord. May You heal the sorrow in their
hearts, let them trust steadfastly in You and let
their hearts rejoice because of Your salvation.
May they sing praises to Your name because
You have dealt bountifully with them. Lord,
may the youth see the beauty that You have
given them, that of a quiet and gentle spirit.
Help them to forgive and bless their enemies
because of what You have done for them.
Thank You that this is possible with You,
God!!!

(Psalm 30:11-12, Psalm 13, Matthew 19:26)

# LIVING WATER

Jesus, we are asking for Your presence to come
over this generation. Daddy let them experience
You for themselves. Let the youth be ones who
will see You and ask You for the living water.
Father, may they be ones who will not let You
pass by, but will plead with You to stay. Jesus,
give them a hunger and a yearning in their hearts
to pursue after You. Father, let the youth
declare that it is no longer because of what
others have said that they believe, for they have
heard for themselves Your voice. Abba, let them
hear a word from You that only You could
know, a word that would compel them to not
only listen to what You have to say, but one they
would tell all their friends and neighbours.
Abba, let them not be ones who make excuses
about how things should be done, but instead
will receive You and worship You in spirit and in
truth. Father, we ask that even if they don't
understand everything in their mind, that they
would receive the kingdom like a child and enter
in with a childlike faith. Daddy, let this
generation be ones who will receive You and
believe You radically. Let them be ones who will
declare from the rooftops that You are Lord and
share what You have done for them! Father, let
many be drawn to You through their testimony.
Daddy, would You encounter the youth, so that
they could know in the deepest part of their
hearts how much You care for them.

(John 4:42, John 4:29, John 4:20-24)

## SONSHIP

Thank You for the youth, Jesus. You have made them so incredibly kind and tenderhearted. Jesus, would You show the youth how to pray for the hurting and the lost, for the orphans and the widows. Jesus, would You show them how to take the pain they have suffered and use it for Your glory knowing that what has been meant for harm, God, You can bring about for good THIS DAY! Grant the youth great JOY as they trust in You, for the joy of the Lord is their strength! We ask that You would show them how to drink from the fountain that never runs dry, the living waters that will flow right through them! Help this generation to watch and pray. Thank You for making them unique in Your image. Let their soul know it full well! Thank You that You have made this generation one of a kind, and we declare over the youth, they are not a mistake, for God, You do not make mistakes! You planned and purposed for them to be here before the foundations of the world and for that we give You praise!

(Ephesians 4:32, Genesis 50:20, Nehemiah 8:10, Mark 14;38, James 1:27, Psalm 139, John 4:4-36)

# DIVINE EXCHANGE

Jesus, thank You that You never forget the youth. Thank You Jesus that this generation is engraved on the palm of Your hand. Pour out Your love on them. Jesus, thank You that You came to make all things new. You did not come to call the righteous, but the sinners to repentance, because the healthy do not need a physician, but the sick do. Abba, would You give the youth eye salve that they might see and let them buy from You gold refined in the fire, so that they can become rich. Thank You that You are the one who turns their mourning into joy and You give them the garment of praise for the spirit of heaviness. Abba, would You comfort the youth and give them gladness for sorrow. Jesus, we are asking that You would heal this generation's heart. Cause their minds to forget trauma from the past. Give them Your peace that passes all understanding, that even their families would see the goodness of God in this generation. We command all trauma to go, in Jesus' name. Let Your healing balm of love come on them. Jesus, thank You that You came to heal the brokenhearted, to proclaim freedom to the captives and the opening of the prison to them that are bound, to proclaim the acceptable year of the Lord and the day of vengeance of our God, to comfort all that mourn, to give them beauty for ashes, the oil of joy for mourning, the garment of praise for the spirit of heaviness. Jesus, cause this generation to be called the trees of righteousness, the planting of the Lord, that

You might be glorified. Thank You that they are ones who will build the old waste places and raise up the former desolations. LORD, they will repair the ruined cities, the desolations of many generations. Thank You Jesus. Everything that has been stolen from them and their families will be fully restored and returned to them in abundance. For every tear, we call in the joy and love of Jesus. For all pain, let there be peace that passes all understanding. Abba, thank You that You are singing a jubilant song over the youth, a song of radical love. Let them hear the song You are singing over them. Let this generation be able to comfort others with the comfort that You have comforted them with, in Jesus' name. Thank You that You are the God of peace, and are with them.

(Isaiah 49:16, Mark 2:17, Revelation 3:18, Jeremiah 31:13, Isaiah 61, Philippians 4:7, Zephaniah 3:17, 2 Corinthians 1:4, 2 Corinthians 13:11)

# TASTE & SEE

Daddy, we thank You for Your extravagant love for the youth. Thank You Abba, that You delight in them, that You will quiet them with Your love, and that You will rejoice over them with singing. Daddy, we ask that You open the youth's ears to hear the song that You are singing over them and open their eyes to see how You are rejoicing over them, how You truly are a Good Father. We speak Psalm 18 over the youth and we thank You, Abba, that when the sound of this generation's voice reaches Your ears, that You are more than ready and more than willing to rescue them. Thank You that You truly will shake heaven and earth and reach down from on high and take hold of them to draw them out of deep waters because You delight in this generation. Thank You, Abba that You have called the youth to greatness, and You have more in store for them than they could even imagine. Let them taste and see of Your goodness, and be forever lost in Who You are, because You have already proved the vastness of Your love for this generation. Abba let them see it, in Jesus' name.

(Zephaniah 3:17, Psalm 18:16, Psalm 34:8)

# MARKED

Jesus, thank You that the youth are marked for You.  Thank You for the call that You have on their lives as a worshippers and ministers of Jesus.  We declare that they are ones who will observe Your word and keep Your covenant.
They will teach Your judgments and Your law.  Thank You that they are ones who will put incense before You and whole burnt sacrifices on Your altar.  Father, let their lives be worship poured out before You.  Teach this generation how to worship and pray to fill the bowls in heaven.  Raise them up to be incense poured out on You and draw them to give their whole life as a sacrifice to You.  Father, we ask for purity in worship and a desire for You, that even the children would long for You more than anything else.  Daddy, would You bless their substance and accept the work of their hands.  Strike the loins of those who rise against them and of those who hate them, that they rise not again.  Jesus, we ask that the enemy would have no power over the youth at all because Your hand is upon them and they have given themselves to You.  Draw them to give their whole selves to You, even as a little children and may they never look back, but walk in the fullness of the calling You have for them!

(Deuteronomy 33:9-10, Deuteronomy 33:11)

# SONSHIP

Abba, thank You for the children. Thank You
that You have called them Your sons and
daughters and that You have sent forth the Spirit
of Your Son into their hearts, crying out, "Abba,
Father!" Thank You that they are ones who will
take You at Your word and dare to believe
You. Jesus, You promised that the kingdom of
heaven belongs to such as these, so we thank
You that the kids will see Your kingdom come
on earth as it is in heaven. Let them be ones who
are consecrated to You and who will not run to
all manner of other things before they give
themselves fully to You. Let them fall so in love
with You even now, Jesus, that You are their one
desire! Let them see You and know You! And
let countless others be drawn to You through the
children, in Jesus' name.

(Galatians 4:6, Psalm 27:4, Matthew 19:14)

# TRUTH

Abba Father, we thank You for the life you have given the children. God, we pray that they will forever be joined to You, that their lives would be a prophetic sign and wonder. LORD, we pray that they would know right from wrong and not go after the world's teaching, but rather that they would desire to know the truth of Your word. LORD, we believe that You will raise up the youth as prophets in their spheres of influence, even at this very young age. We declare over them that as they begin to declare the word of the LORD, that others will tune in to what they are saying and abide in the decrees that You make through them. We declare over this generation that no one will look down on them because they are young but that this generation will set an example for other believers, in Jesus' name!

(Deuteronomy 18:15, 1 Timothy 4:12)

# CHOSEN

Jesus, thank You that You chose the Levites to minister to You in the temple. You chose them to minister to You forever. Thank You Jesus, that the youth are a chosen generation, a royal people, Your own special people, who are called to show forth the praises of Him who called them out of the darkness and into Your marvelous light. Thank You that they are clearly marked for greatness in Your kingdom. Jesus, we ask that the youth would not be hindered from coming to You and hearing You at the age they are right now. Let them be like Samuel who was chosen even before birth to serve You and minister before You and lead Your people in righteousness. Let them, like Samuel, hear You, recognize Your voice, and fully obey You no matter what the cost. Let them even now walk in the call You have for them as worshipers of the King; to remember what You have done, to thank and to praise You, and to simply worship You for who You are. Jesus, let Your grace and peace be multiplied to them in the knowledge of God and of Jesus our Lord. Thank You that You have called this generation to walk in holiness and righteousness from childhood and that many will see that it is one marked for the King. We decree, "Youth, you are pledged to the King and no one else." Make them one with You, Jesus. Let them know You.

(1 Chronicles 15:2, 1 Peter 2:9, 1 Samuel 1:11,
1 Samuel 3:1-21, 1 Chronicles 16:4, 2 Peter 1:2-3,
John 17:23)

DAY 284

# NEW CREATION

Abba, we thank You that if the youth are in Christ they are new creations. Even at this young age, the old sin nature falls off, and You have made them new in Your image. Father, we decree over them that they are ones who hear the voice of God and are endowed with great wisdom. The youth will have a holy dread of God that will keep them from stumbling; they will forever see You before their eyes. They will not flatter themselves, but will run with the identity of King Jesus. The youth will see sin and hate it and be filled with mercy and compassion for the lost. LORD, we pray that even if everyone else around them are filled with words of malice and deception, they will act wisely and will do good to the glory of God. Even on their beds this generation will dream of You rather than making malicious and deceptive plans. They will long to set their feet on the path of life, where Jesus is the lamp to their feet and they will reject evil.

(2 Corinthians 5:17, Psalm 36:1-4, Psalm 119:105, Psalm 97:10)

# BONDSERVANT

Father, we decree that this generation is one that is pledged to You. We declare that they will so long to be with the King and serve the King, that even when they have opportunity to walk away they will pierce their ear to the door saying, "No, I am a bondservant of the King forever. I choose Jesus. I choose to stay." Father, we ask that You would raise up the youth as ones who will see the beauty of loving only Jesus! We declare that they are called to be sent ones of Jesus Christ by the will of God, not from man nor through man, but through Jesus Christ! We declare that they are bondservants of Jesus Christ. Father, we ask that even as children they would be ones to whom it is given to know the mysteries of the kingdom of heaven, so that hearing they may not only hear but understand, and seeing they may not only see but perceive. Father, we ask that You would raise them up, even as a young men and women, to be ones who are instructed concerning the kingdom of heaven, who bring out treasures to share with those around them. Holy Spirit, would You teach them, so that they can pull out the treasures of the kingdom for others! We declare understanding over the youth that every seed of the word that is sown will grow and bear fruit. In Jesus' name.

(1 Corinthians 6:17, 1 Corinthians 1:1, Galatians 1:1, Philippians 1:1, Matthew 13:11-15, Matthew 13:52, Matthew 13:19)

## FAITH

Abba, let this generation be one who has great faith and will take the little bit of oil that You have given them and run with it.  That they will be ones who obey You even when it seems impossible or looks silly.  Let them be ones who see the sick and hurting and lead them to Jesus for healing.  Use them LORD to show others how to walk in the more that You have for them.  Abba, thank You for the great faith that You are growing in the youth and that they are ones who will not be satisfied until the dreams and promises You have given them have come to maturity and have been fully fulfilled.  Jesus, we pray that the youth  will grab a hold of the promises You have given them.  Call them out until they come to life.  We pray they will be ones who will have faith to take what they have been given and see the miracle and potential in it and use it, so that many can be fed with the goodness of the Lord.

(2 Kings 4:1-7, 2 Kings 4:42-44, 2 Kings 5:3,
2 Kings 5:8-37)

# HEARING GOD

Thank You so much for the plans and purposes
You have for the youth.  You have called them
to hold a plumb line of righteousness before the
foundations of the earth!  Jesus, we pray that
they would be dedicated to Your service and to
Your will.  May they hear Your voice so clearly
and so precisely that nothing would move them!
Let none of  their words fall to the ground.
Jesus, would You create such a boldness in this
generation to proclaim Your word with all the
power and authority that You have given them,
as it is written, "The righteous are as bold as a
lion".  Your word says that, "My sheep hear my
voice and they will not follow another".  Thank
You that You are training the youth now to hear
and follow You.  Send them ones to encourage
them, and let them know that they are not
alone.  Thank You that You will never leave nor
forsake them, Papa!

(1 Samuel 3:1-19, 1 Kings 19:18, Hebrews 13:5)

DAY 288

## BOLDNESS

Jesus, we ask that You take this generation to a whole new level of boldness. Abba, make them the ones who won't care about the opinions of man, but that they will hear Your heartbeat and run with it. Father, we ask that You give them a voice to proclaim Your goodness, where it may have been stolen in the past, we demand a seven-fold return for them. Let the youth be the ones, Jesus, who are so wrecked for You that they truly cannot help but speak the things that they have seen and heard. Draw them, Abba. Let them taste and see of Your goodness, and be so undone by You that You would be their one heart's desire. May they cry out, "One thing I have desired of the LORD, that will I seek: that I may dwell in the house of the LORD all the days of my life, to behold the beauty of the LORD, and to inquire in His temple."

(Acts 4:20, Psalm 27:4)

# PRESENCE

Abba would You raise the youth up as ones who are fully given to You. As young men and women who care about the things of the Lord, that they may be holy both in body and in spirit. Thank You for the calling of purity that You have on their lives and we ask that You would show them the beauty of being youth given only to You, and not to another. Give them great joy in Your presence. Let them be the Marys who love to sit at your feet for hours learning from You, Jesus. Quicken them, O God! Would You redeem the time for the youth, and bring them into the fullness of who You have called them to be. Let this be a generation of ones who pour their lives out on You like perfume, and their whole house will be filled with that fragrance! Thank You that this generation is one that brings You great joy!

(1 Corinthians 7:34, John 12:3)

# FAITHFULNESS

Jesus, we thank You for Your very great and
precious promises over the youth; ones born of
God! Thank You that all old things are to pass
away and behold ALL things are to become
new! Thank You that You do not hold our
trespasses against us, rather You give us the
message of reconciliation! That's amazing,
God! We speak over the youth, "Do not fear,
for God is with you; do not be dismayed, for He
is Your God! He will uphold you with His
righteous right hand, and will never leave you
nor forsake you. For His faithfulness will be
your shield and buckler, you will not have to be
afraid for the terror by night; nor the arrow that
flies by day." Even though a thousand may fall
at their side and ten thousand at their right hand,
it will not come near them. Thank You that You
have been protecting this generation since the
foundations of the earth, and have loved them
and chosen them to be blameless and holy in
Your sight, O God! Thank You that You have
given the youth a voice for their people, so we
pray that You would raise them up for such a
time is this! We thank You for love that never
ends! AMEN.

(Isaiah 41:10, 2 Corinthians 5:17-19, Psalm 91:5-7,
Ephesians 1:4, Esther 4:14,1 Corinthians 13:8)

# WORSHIP

Father, thank You for the worshippers You are
raising up in this generation. We pray that You
would draw them to Your heart, that they would
so fall in love with You that nothing else would
matter to them anymore. Jesus, we ask that You
would become so precious to the young men and
women of this generation that they would even
break their most precious possession over You
and pour it out at Your feet. We decree that the
worshippers will bring You great pleasure, and
cause Your heart to skip a beat simply by their
love for You! Raise them up as a worshippers
who will see battles shifted and won simply by
giving You glory. Teach this generation how to
war in praise, standing still and seeing the
salvation of the Lord. Jesus, we ask that they
would continue to press in, in praise, and that
they would see the enemy defeated in their
families, their schools, and their homes. We
declare that the youth are a warriors who will not
give up, but will bring You great joy in simple
worship, and simple obedience.

(2 Chronicles 20:21-22, Matthew 26:7,
Song of Solomon 4:9)

# OVERCOMER

Abba, thank You for these chosen youth. Overcomers. Overcomers. Overcomers. Jesus, thank You that You make ALL things new; that whoever is in Christ is a new creation. We ask, Jesus, that You would make this generation completely new; nothing old left, not a desire or craving or thought; ALL brand new. Show them the power of the cross; that the cross brings life and freedom. Thank You that whom the Son sets free is FREE INDEED!!! We declare the freedom of Christ over the youth. Thank You that they are ones who will flee youthful passions and pursue righteousness, faith, love and peace along with those who call on the Lord from pure hearts. Wreck the youth for Your kingdom, Holy Spirit. Open their eyes to hate the yuck of sin and see Your incredible sacrifice. Jesus, we ask that the youth would be firmly grounded, wearing Your full armor - the belt of truth, the breastplate of righteousness, the helmet of salvation, the shoes of the gospel of peace, and the sword of the Spirit - so that they would be able to withstand all the flaming arrows of the devil. Thank You for the warriors that the children are. Thank You that like Gideon, no matter how insignificant any one of them feels, You will use them to crush the enemy and set Your people free - their generation. Thank You that the youth are a force to contend with and that with You they cannot be stopped.

(Psalm 18:29, 2 Corinthians 5:17, John 8:36,
2 Timothy 2:22, Ephesians 6:10-20)

# SEEK

Thank You Jesus that You have marked this generation, chosen them and set them apart. Thank You that the good work that You started in each youth, You will also be faithful to complete. So we ask, Abba, that You draw the youth to Yourself and give them revelation of Your heart toward them. Father, we pray that You put a drive in them to call out for insight and cry aloud for understanding; to look for it as for silver and search for it as for hidden treasure, that they may understand the fear of the LORD and find the knowledge of God. Place in them an urgency to seek You fervently while You may yet be found. Thank You that You promised that those who search for You with all their heart will find You, in Jesus name.

(Philippians 1:6, Proverbs 2:3-5, Jeremiah 29:13)

## FREEDOM

Thank You Jesus for Your hand upon the children. Thank You for the incredible purpose and call that You have for each one of them. Jesus, we ask that You would come heal them and set them free. Jesus, You said that You are the Spirit and where the Spirit of the Lord is, there is freedom. Father, we ask that the youth would turn to You and that the veil would be taken away. We declare that they are ones who will, with unveiled faces, behold as in a mirror the glory of the Lord, and will be transformed into the same image from glory to glory. Daddy, would You draw them to Your heart. Jesus, we ask that their minds would no longer be blinded by the god of this age, but that the light of the gospel of the glory of Christ, the image of God, would shine on them!!! Jesus, You are the God who commanded light to shine out of darkness, so Father we ask that You would also shine into the hearts of the children to give them the light of the knowledge of the glory of God in the face of Jesus Christ. Jesus, You are the light that shone in the darkness, and the darkness could not comprehend You. Would You shine on this generation. Thank You that Your light is stronger than any darkness.

(2 Corinthians 3:16-18, 2 Corinthians 4:3-6, John 1:5)

# BLAMELESS

Jesus, thank You for Your incredible love for children. Jesus, we ask that they would sing of your steadfast love and justice. Let them ponder the way that is blameless. Let them walk with integrity of heart within their houses; let them determine in their hearts that they will not set before their eyes anything that is worthless. Let them HATE the work of those who fall away; that it will not cling to them. Set a perverse heart far from them that they will know nothing of evil. Thank You that You look with favor on the faithful in the land, so that they may dwell with You. Let this generation be one that is faithful and will dwell with You. Let the youth walk in the way that is blameless and be ones who will minister to You, because no one who practices deceit shall dwell in Your house, and no one who utters lies shall continue before Your eyes. Thank You, Jesus, that these children will be truthful, honest and trustworthy; men and women of integrity. Train them to be faithful in the little things so that You can trust them with much. Thank You, Jesus, that like Daniel, these will be youth without blemish, of good appearance and skillful in all wisdom, endowed with knowledge and understanding, learning and competent to stand in the king's palace and able to learn the literature and language of the kingdom.

(Psalm 101, Luke 16:10, Daniel 1:4)

DAY 296

# CALLING

Jesus, thank You for the youth! Thank You that You created them and called them from the womb. Father, thank You that You have called each one by name from before they were even born. We declare that the children's mouths are like sharp swords, speaking the very words of God! We declare that the youth are hidden in the shadow of Your hand; ones who abide in Your secret place. We say that this generation is a polished shaft hidden in Your quiver. Father, we ask that You train their hands for war and their fingers to fight. We ask that the youth would have soft hearts to allow You to polish them and make them the sword You have created them to be. Abba, You created the youth to be Your servants in whom You will be glorified. You created them to be Your servants who will bring the lost back to You, so that they can be gathered to You. Father, You created this generation to be glorious in Your eyes, and You promise that You will be their strength. Would You give the children a great hunger to cry out for discernment and for understanding, to seek for her as silver and as for hidden treasure because You promise that then they will understand the fear of the Lord, and find the knowledge of God. May they listen to You because from Your mouth come knowledge and understanding. Draw this generation, O God!!! Thank You for the incredible calling You have for them!!

(Isaiah 49:1-5, Proverbs 2:3-6, Psalm 144:1)

# PURITY

LORD, we lift up this generation to You. Holy Spirit, please teach them how to cleanse themselves and how to totally once and for all remove all evil from their lives and nail it to the cross. Please teach them how to do what is good, to seek justice, to deal with corruption, to defend the rights of the oppressed and fatherless and to plead the widow's cause. LORD, Your word says that if the youth come and discuss these things with You that though their sins are like scarlet, they will be as white as snow; though they are as red as crimson, they will be like wool. Father, Your heart's cry over the youth is that if they are willing and obedient, they will eat the good things of the land, but if they refuse the cross they will stay in utter rebellion, which will cause them to be devoured by the sword. LORD, clear the path of these ones, so that they can clearly see the road to You and blow on them so that they will run after You, Jesus!

(Isaiah 1:16-20)

# SONSHIP

"'Therefore come out from them, and be separate,' says the Lord. 'Touch no unclean thing and I will receive you.' And, 'I will be a Father to you, and you will be My sons and daughters,' says the Lord Almighty." Abba, thank You that You see the youth as Your sons and daughters. We pray that You would reveal Your Father heart of love to them, that each one will know and live in the fullness of the power of Your almighty love. Thank You that You are calling them apart from the world. Teach them not to keep striving to be like the world, when You have clearly called them out of that thing. Thank You that You promise to receive each one. Thank You for Your identity in this generation. Would You begin to reveal it now. Thank You that You are calling the youth to be Your bride. We declare in faith that this is the generation that will make itself ready for the King. That these ones will be clothed in white with their lamps burning when the marriage supper of the Lamb comes. Thank You, Jesus. Call out the youth, Abba. Draw them to Yourself, so that they can know You. Where their faith has been crushed, let it come alive again. Thank You, Jesus. Amen.

(2 Corinthians 6:17, Romans 12:2, Matthew 25:1-13, John 6:44)

# ROOTED IN LOVE

Thank You, Jesus, for these youth. Father,
would You let them behold You, and be wooed
and won by Your extravagant love for them.
Lord, we pray that You would grant them,
according to the riches of Your glory, to be
strengthened with might through Your Spirit in
the inner man, so that Christ may dwell in their
hearts through faith. Also, that they, being
rooted and grounded in love, may be able to
comprehend with all the saints what is the width
and length and depth and height - to know the
love of Christ which passes knowledge, so the
youth may be filled with all the fullness of
God. Now to You, Abba, who is able to do
exceedingly abundantly above all that they can
even ask or think, according to the power that
works in them, to You be glory in the church by
Christ Jesus to all generations, forever. Abba, let
these young men and women be so undone by
Your love that they are truly wrecked for all
eternity! Mat they count all things loss for the
excellence of the knowledge of Christ Jesus, so
that they can gain You, and be found in You, not
having their own righteousness, which is from
the law, but that which is through faith in Christ,
the righteousness which is from God by faith;
that they may know You, and the power of Your
resurrection, and the fellowship of Your
sufferings, being conformed to Your death.
Thank You that You are not done with them yet,
in Jesus' name!

(Ephesians 3:16-21, Philippians 3:8-11)

# LIFE

Thank You Jesus for the youth.  Father thank
You for what You are doing in their hearts in
wooing and drawing them.  We speak life over
them, where they have felt dry and dead and not
sure why nothing seems to be working.  Father
let Your life come now!  Let them come alive
with passion for You!  Jesus You said that
whoever eats Your flesh and drinks Your blood
has eternal life, and You will raise him up at the
last day.  Father we ask that You would give this
generation a ravenous hunger for You, to devour
You and Your word, and have Your life fill
them, because apart from eating and drinking of
You, we have no life.  Abba, we're asking that
they would come to You and feast on You,
abiding in You, and You in them.  Jesus You
promised that those who feed on You will live
because of You, and will live forever.  Jesus
would You teach them how to feed on You, so
that they can live.  We speak life over their whole
families.  Father let Your saving grace come
now, in Jesus' name!

(Luke 15:32, John 6:53-58)

# ADOPTION

Lord we pray that in You the youth will know the
richness of Your Spirit of adoption; that they
would intimately know the depths of Your love
and Your suffering; that their greatest desire
among people would be to know nothing, but the
mysteries of Christ and Him crucified.  May they
know that overcoming each trial is worth it,
loving beyond reason is worth it, forgiving
without measure is worth it, turning the other
cheek is worth it and suffering for doing good is
commendable before God.

(Romans 8:15, 1 Corinthians 2:2, Matthew 6:14,
Matthew 5:39, 1 Peter 3:17)

## INTIMACY

Thank You Jesus that You are strengthening the youth's hands for war and their fingers for battle.  Let them not be afraid or dismayed Abba, for You are with them, and it is Your battle not theirs.  Thank You Jesus that in our weakness You show Yourself strong.  Thank You that as the youth wait on You they will renew their strength; that they will mount up on wings like eagles, they will run and not grow weary, they will walk and not faint.  You are so much greater than everything, Daddy.  Thank You that You are always sufficient; that You are more than enough.  Abba we ask that in this season You would teach them to rest in You, even in the midst of the battle; that they would have such a childlike trust in You that they can be sleeping in the boat even when the storm is raging all around them.  We ask even for an increase of secret place time with You Daddy, to cultivate unshakable intimacy like what Jesus had, and to search out the secrets of Your heart.  Abba Your heart is so beating for the youth!  Let them hear it!

(Psalm 144:1, Joshua 1:9, 2 Corinthians 12:9, Isaiah 40:31, Matthew 8:24)

# HOLINESS

Jesus we thank You that You are readying this generation's mind for action. Thank You that You are revealing the seriousness of the hour we are in to them and that they are setting their hope completely on the grace that You are bringing to them at the revelation of Jesus Christ. LORD, we thank You that the youth are growing in obedience to the cross and are being transformed into the image of Christ. Jesus You are holy and You have called the youth to be holy through Your blood that was spilled, so that they can be free from the bonds of sin. LORD help them to conduct themselves in the fear of the LORD during their temporary time of residence here on earth, for You have redeemed them and they are no longer bound by the path of carnality, for You redeemed them by the precious blood of Jesus. You did this, so that their faith and hope would be in You.

(1 Peter 1:13-21)

## PURITY

Jesus we lift up the children before You.  Thank You that they are ones who will stand spotless and pure before You.  Thank You that they are called to be a part of Your bride who will make themselves ready for the King.  They are ones who will be glad and rejoice at Your coming. Thank You Jesus for the fullness of Your grace filling this generation.  Thank You God that You are able to make all grace abound toward them and that they always have all sufficiency in all things, and an abundance for every good work. Let them never lack anything of the fullness of what You have for them.  Let them be ones who will abide in You all the time.  We pray they will abide in the vine and bear much fruit.

(Revelation 19:7, 2 Corinthians 9:8, John 15:4-5)

# INTIMACY

Thank You Daddy, that the youth are overcomers. Thank You that they are ones who won't quit until they find the truth. Father we ask that You would draw them to Your heart; that even in the busyness of ministry, Your affections toward them would draw them into an intimacy with You that they have never known before. When You say to them, "Seek my face," let their heart's response to You be, "Your face, Lord, I will seek." Father we pray that in this season You would knit their hearts to Yours, that the desires of Your heart become the desires of their hearts, and that their heart's cry would be, "One thing I have desired of the LORD, that will I seek: that I may dwell in the house of the LORD all the days of my life, to behold the beauty of the LORD, and to inquire in His temple." Would You open up time for them to sit with You and lean their heads against Your chest, listening to your heartbeat. Thank You that Your sheep hear Your voice, and You know them and they follow You, so would You reveal the mysteries of your heart to the children. Reveal to them Your kingdom strategies, that everything they put their hands to would have Your heart behind it. Thank You for this generation and for how You are using them, and thank You that this is just the beginning for them--the best is yet to come!

(Psalm 27:8, Psalm 27:4, John 10:27)

# PRESENCE

Abba, thank You for the youth. Thank You for
how incredibly You designed each one of
them. Thank You that the youth are not what
they do, but who they are. We break off any lie
right now, that says that the youth are only worth
what they do. Thank You that they are Your
priceless treasures. Jesus, thank You that Your
desire is that these ones would be with You
where You are and see Your glory, because You
loved them from the foundation of the world.
Jesus, let the youth know their priceless value, so
that everything they do will flow from a place of
knowing their identity. May they drink of the
fullness of You, so that out of their innermost
being will flow rivers of living water to everyone
around them. Let them be like Moses, who
never desired to leave Your presence, but that
they would long to see Your glory. Nothing less
than You will be good enough for them. Only
You can satisfy. Jesus, no matter if they are at
home or away, may each one on their own seek
out Your presence until they find You. Let them
long rather to be a doorkeeper in the house of
the Lord than to dwell in the tents of the wicked,
because they have tasted that better is one day in
Your courts than a thousand elsewhere. Let the
children be ones who will lead many others into
Your presence, even like Moses took Joshua and
seventy others into Your presence and they ate
and drank with You.

(John 17:24, Exodus 33:15, Psalm 27:4, Psalm 84:10)

# WARRIOR

Thank You Jesus that this generation is destined for greatness. Thank You that Your plans for them are beyond even their wildest dreams! Abba, would You teach them to lead; even at their young ages, that they would learn how to lead with honour, and lead well. Thank You that they WILL set an example for the believers. Abba, thank You that the youth are stand-takers, even like Daniel, Shadrach, Meshach and Abednego. We ask, Jesus, would You so establish Your precepts inside them that no matter what law, society or status quo says, that they will never bow to anything, but the King of kings and Lord of lords and in so doing, that they will pave the way for entire nations to follow them into righteousness and holiness. Teach them to count the cost, Abba, but let them not be afraid, knowing that You are the Treasure in the field, and really are worth giving everything for. Thank You that You Yourself will teach the children; that they don't need anybody else to teach them because You are revealing the mysteries of Your heart to each one of them. Jesus, we ask that You keep them hidden under the shadow of Your wings; that the enemy not even be able to find them, in Jesus' name.

(1 Timothy 4:12, Matthew 13:44, John 14:26, Psalm 17:8)

# AUTHORITY

Jesus, thank You that this generation will
burning for You. Thank You that You are
igniting a fire in the youth that nothing will be
able to quench. We ask, Jesus, that each one
would study to show themselves approved to
God, a workman who does not need to be
ashamed, rightly dividing the word of truth. Let
them follow You, Holy Spirit, and not what
other people say, so that they would lead from a
place of intimacy with the Father. We proclaim
the youth are not ones who will be tossed about
by the wind, but they will know the truth and the
truth will set them free- free to live and be love
in You. They will be ones who receive the things
that they ask of God in faith. Thank You that
the youth are ones who will see the power and
authority of God flowing through them
firsthand, because they will know the authority
that is available to them in Christ; the youth will
lay hands on the sick and see them recover, they
will see the dead raised and the lepers cleansed,
they will see blind eyes and deaf ears open, they
will have a faith that can move mountains, but it
will not be in vain because it is filled with the
love of God. Thank You Jesus, that more than
anything else the youth will be like Mary and
pour their worship and their lives on loving and
adoring You, Jesus, no matter how many people
think that it is useless. Jesus, You are honored
when the children love You with all their hearts
and all their souls, all their minds and all their
strengths. Jesus, thank You that this will be a

generation of good Bereans. They will know the truth for themselves directly from You and their foundation will be set upon a Rock. Thank You that they will know the truth because each one has a deep relationship with You, spends hours in Your presence with You, and the oil that they have gathered and the good thing that they have chosen- no one will take away from them.

(2 Timothy 2:15, James 1:7, Matthew 21:22,
1 Corinthians 13, John 12:3)

## FAITH

Thank You, Jesus, for an unshakable faith for this generation. Let them hear the word, so that faith may grow in them. Jesus let the youth be ones who will simply believe You and who will see the impossible because they know the God of the impossible. Raise them up, Daddy! Let them know the joyful sound and let them walk, O LORD, in the light of Your countenance. In Your name, let them rejoice all day long and in Your righteousness, they will be exalted. Teach the youth Your way, O LORD. Let them walk in Your truth. Unite their hearts to fear Your name and let them praise You, Jesus, with all their hearts!

(Psalm 89:15-16, Psalm 86:11-12)

# PURITY

Father thank You so much for the youth. We declare that they are ones who are pure in heart who will see God. Father we ask that this generation would be one that has clean hands and a pure heart, that they would give their hearts and their worship and their attention to only You and no other. Father we ask that they would be ones who would give You their yes in truth and do everything that You have put on their hearts to do. Father You promise that those are the ones who may ascend onto the hill of the Lord and stand in Your holy place. Father we declare that these are ones who will so value being with You that anything that comes in the way will be counted as wickedness to them. Father would You show them how to pursue holiness, that they may see You. Thank You Jesus that You are the One Who gave Yourself for us to sanctify and cleanse us and present us glorious, having no spot or wrinkle or any such thing! We declare that this is a generation who will believe God and it will be counted to them as righteousness.

(Matthew 5:8, Psalm 24:3-5, Hebrews 12:14,
Ephesians 5:25-27, Romans 4:3)

# MESSENGER

Father we lift up this generation to You and pray
that they will be messengers who will clear the
way before You, so that the LORD, Your people
are seeking, will suddenly come to His temple;
the Messenger of the covenant we all desire -
God You have declared He is coming!  Father
we pray that the children would be able to
endure the day of Your return, for You will
come this time as the Refiner's Fire and like
cleansing lye.  You will come and purify like gold
and silver.  May they be refined now and present
their offerings to You in righteousness
now!  LORD teach them how to offer offerings
that will please You!  Fill them with the fear of
the LORD, O God.

(Malachi 3:1-5)

# STRONG & COURAGEOUS

Jesus, thank You for these amazing young men
and women of God! We thank You for how
incredibly You made them. Thank You that
they are mountain movers. Thank You, Jesus,
that You promised that if Your people have faith
like a mustard seed, they will say to mountains,
'move from here to there,' and they will move,
and nothing will be impossible for them. Thank
You, Jesus, that the youth will be ones who are
not satisfied with status quo and will not bend
simply because of someone else's opinion, but
they will hear what You say to them and run with
it- no turning back. Thank You that they are
courageous and valiant, and that each one causes
the enemy to tremble. Thank You that they are
fearless warriors. Like Joshua, they will go in
and take the land. Even in their schools, they
will go in fearlessly and claim it for Your
kingdom. The youth will be strong and
courageous. They will not be terrified or
dismayed- for You, Lord, will be their God, and
You are with them wherever they go.

(Matthew 17:20, Joshua 1:9)

## MIGHTY WARRIOR

Abba, thank You that You take the weak ones and You do something AMAZING!!! You take the misfits, and You raise them up as mighty warriors! Jesus, would You do so with the youth. Please protect them and keep them humble. As You have them doing the things that may seem insignificant, may You encourage each one that those are the things that move the very heart of God! Thank You, Jesus, that You can do above and beyond what we can ask or imagine!!! Would each one continue to build trust in You as You are raising them up. Let them know that You love them, give them wisdom, and grant them patience as they grow into who You have called them to be! In Jesus' name Amen!!!

(Matthew 23:12, 1 Samuel 22:2, Ephesians 1:17)

# SENT ONE

Thank You Jesus for our youth. Thank You that they are chosen and called out for such a time as this. Thank You that before You formed any of them in the womb, You knew them; before they were born You sanctified them. You ordained them as prophets to the nations. Jesus, we ask that the youth would be ones who would not be afraid to speak what You have told them. Thank You that they are ones who will carry Your message and gospel to the ends of the earth without fear. We declare over each one, "Do not say, 'I am just a youth.'" For they will go to all to whom Jesus sends them and whatever the Father commands them, they will speak. These youth are ones who will not be afraid for God is with them to deliver them. No more excuses of being too young! Raise each one up to be an example to their generation of young men and women who go after You with everything. Thank You that they are ones who are useful to You in ministry! Thank You that they are not insignificant, but are a mighty force in the kingdom!!!

(Jeremiah 1:3, Jeremiah 1:7-8, 1 Timothy 4:12, 2 Timothy 4:11)

## WARRIOR

Thank You, Jesus, that You give the youth the courage to be able to stand up for righteousness against ungodly religious systems, mobs and authorities with great love, honor and grace. Thank You, Jesus, that we can call forth the youth of our generation as good soldiers for Jesus. Let them be strengthened by the grace that is in You. What they have heard from You let them entrust to faithful men who will be able to teach others also. Teach them to share in Your suffering as good soldiers of Christ Jesus. Let each one be a true soldier who does not get entangled in civilian pursuits, since their aim is to please the one who enlisted them--the Father. Jesus, would You give the youth understanding in everything. Fill them with Your grace. Let them be men and women of grace, love, integrity, purity, and faith. In Jesus' name. Amen.

(2 Timothy 2:1-7)

# FEARLESS

Father, we thank You that the youth will be ones who are bold and courageous, who will not be afraid or dismayed because You are with them wherever they go.  Thank You that everywhere that their feet tread, that there You have given them the land.  We pray, Abba, that each youth will love You so well, that they can actually behold You, and actually speak with You as a man speaks to his friend, like Moses, that they will be ones who will be able to take the seventy with them onto the mountaintop to truly behold You; to eat and drink with You, and feast of your goodness!  Give them revelation of Who You are, Abba!  Raise them up to love You, to love You well, and in so doing, that they would lead entire nations into Your glory, in Jesus' name!

(Joshua 1:9, Joshua 1:3, Exodus 33:11, Exodus 24:9-11)

# FEAR OF THE LORD

God, we thank You that You will use these ones
to instill the fear of God in others; even by the
way they live their lives in honour of You, Jesus.
Lord, use them to purify Your bride, that they
would be used as the crossroads of whether
people choose righteousness or wickedness. We
do pray that those whom You have called would
choose righteousness and, Abba, we pray that
You would protect the youth's hearts if some
don't. Lord let them see Your glory come, let it
not pass them by. Let Your glory come! May
you be honoured and glorified, O GOD!

(Deuteronomy 2:25, Isaiah 40:3, Isaiah 42:6)

# CONSECRATED

Father, thank You for how You are drawing the youth and carrying them close to Your heart. Thank You that Your sheep hear Your voice, so we ask that You open this generation's ears to clearly hear You.  Even at young ages, Abba, let them be like Samuels for their generation, hearing the word of the LORD and declaring it fearlessly, calling their generation back to the plumb line of God!  Even in the night watch, Jesus, would You reveal to them the mysteries of Your heart, that it would not take them years and years to learn, but that they will be taught by the LORD.  Right from the start let them be consecrated to You in holiness and righteousness, ministering to Your heart.  Jesus, You said that the kingdom of heaven belongs ones who are like children, so we ask that the youth will be ones who are like children and will see Your kingdom come, in Jesus' name!

(1 Samuel 3, Isaiah 40:11, Isaiah 54:13, Matthew 6:10)

## SENT

This is what the LORD says, "Stand at the crossroads and look; ask for the ancient paths, ask where the good way is, and walk in it, and you will find rest for your souls." Father, we pray the youth will respond to You by saying, "I will walk in it. Send me I will go." Father, we pray that they will declare this to their generation and to those in their schools and in later years their work places - anywhere their feet tread. May this generation proclaim this among the nations. We declare You are consecrating them for war; stirring up the mighty ones. Let all the people of war draw near; let them come up. LORD teach them to beat their plowshares into swords, and their pruning hooks into spears. Let the weak say, "I am a strong."

(Jeremiah 6:16, Joel 3:9-10)

# SOLD OUT

Abba, thank You so much for how amazing You created the youth.  Thank You for the compassion that You have given them.  Thank You that these are ones who will see the lonely, hurting, fatherless and broken, and radiate Your love to them.  Let them be moved with Your compassion, Jesus, to heal the sick and bring life to the broken and dying.  Thank You, Jesus, that the youth are a city on a hill that will not be hidden no matter how hard anyone tries to hide them under a basket; that Your light will burst out of them, the Father's love will overflow out of them and Your rivers of living water will spring up in them into everlasting life.  Thank You Jesus.  Pour out Your Abba love on them, that the fullness of the love that You have for Jesus might be in them and You in them.  Thank You that this generation is not a quitter, but an overcomer.  Jesus, we also ask that You would surround the youth, so that they would know that they are not alone.  Let them be strong and courageous; not be terrified or afraid for You are with them wherever they go.  Let Your favor and blessing be on whatever they put their hands to, in Jesus name.  Thank You Jesus, that these are ones who will obey You to the end, who will pick up their cross and follow You; that like Peter they will say, "Where else should we go?  You have the words of eternal life."

(Matthew 5:14, Matthew 14:14, John 7:38, John 4:14, John 17:26, Joshua 1:9, Deuteronomy 28:8, John 6:68, John 16:24)

# NEW CREATION

Father, we declare over this generation that they are sons and daughters who will not despise the discipline of the Lord, and will not be discouraged when rebuked by You, but that they are ones whom the Lord loves, that's why they are disciplined, and they are sons who are received by the Father.  Father, we ask that as You draw the youth that they would not despise Your correction, but that they will see it as an opportunity to grow and be more like You.  Father, may they be excited to get rid of the things You are asking them to, knowing that they are hearing You, and following after You.  Jesus, we ask that they would be in subjection to the Father and live.  Thank You, Abba, that You chasten the youth for their profit, that they may be partakers of Your holiness.  Thank You for the peaceable fruit of righteousness that is coming in the youth as a result of being trained by You.  Father, we ask that they would be ones who listen to You and it is their greatest joy to obey You.  We declare that this is a generation who will live, and be partakers of the holiness of God.  In Jesus' name!

(Hebrews 12:5-11, Hebrews 12:5-6)

# HOLINESS

Jesus we thank You so much for the lives of the youth. We thank You that You are using them to increase Your kingdom here on earth. We declare over the youth, "You are imitators of Christ, beloved children; walk in love, just as Christ also loved you and gave Himself up for you as an offering and sacrifice to God as a fragrant aroma." Father we pray for the full liberation of this generation, so that immorality or any impurity or greed will not even be named among them, as is proper for the saints. LORD place a coal upon their lips, so that their speech will be clean, sensible, important, soft refined and filled with thanksgiving. LORD raise up the youth to declare the truth of Your word, not just because of the call of God on their lives, but because they have a rich and deep love for You. LORD we thank You that You have proclaimed from the foundation of the world that You have called the children to inherit the kingdom of Christ and God. Holy Spirit, please protect the youth from those who would try to deceive them with empty words and open their eyes to see those who would try to lead them astray. We declare that the enemy has no hold on the youth because God is drawing them into the light and the darkness is fleeing from them. Holy Spirit we ask that You empower this generation to walk as a children of Light, for the fruit of Light consists in all goodness and righteousness and truth; help them to try and learn what is pleasing to the LORD. God we declare that this generation has been called to not participate in the unfruitful deeds of darkness, but instead to expose them. LORD, as the youth expose the darkness these things will become visible and Your light will infiltrate the ground. Awake, awake children of God and rise from the dead and Christ will shine on you. Send Your angelic host to help the youth in their walk as a wise sons and daughters, making the most of their time because these days are evil and in need of heroes of the faith to rise up.

(Ephesians 5:1-17)

# RIGHTEOUSNESS

Jesus, we thank You that Your word over this generation will not return to You void, but it will accomplish what You please, and will prosper in the thing for which You sent it. Let it come now, in Jesus' name! Rain down, you heavens from above and let the skies pour down righteousness; let the earth open, let them bring forth salvation, and let righteousness spring up together. You the LORD have created it. Jesus, would You crucify the youth with You, so that it is no longer they who live, but You living in them. Grant them repentance, Jesus, so they can live! Thank You that You are the Way, the Truth and the Life. Abba, let the youth and children seek You while You may be found; search for You as for hidden treasure. Thank You Jesus, that once this generation gets it, they will truly be unstoppable and untouchable because You are with them! We declare over this generation, "The Lord is with you, Mighty men and women of Valor; go in this might of yours, for the Lord has sent you! Be strong and courageous, do not be afraid or dismayed, for the LORD your God is with you wherever you go."

(Isaiah 45:8, Galatians 2:20, John 14:6, Judges 6:12-14, Joshua 1:9)

DAY 324

## WATCHMEN

DAY 325

Jesus, thank You so much for the children and for the incredible call You have on each one of their lives. Jesus, thank You that right now You are not sending them to a people of foreign speech and hard language; You are calling them to their own generation to be the watchman on the wall and to sound Your alarm. God we ask that You would make their faces harder than flint, so that no matter if people listen to them or not, these will know that they are called by the Father, they are loved by the Father and this generation will not compromise or disobey You, Abba, on account of any persecution or trouble, in Jesus' name. Let them eat Your word and let it be sweet in their mouths and their stomachs.

(Ezekiel 3:3-5, Ezekiel 33:7, Ezekiel 3:9)

# IDENTITY

Father thank You so much for the youth. Abba
thank You that they are chosen and set apart by
You. Father may these ones be planted on the
mountain height and be ones to bring forth
boughs, and bear fruit, and be like majestic
cedars. Abba we decree that the youth will be a
refuge to those around them and will create
relief for those who are stuck in addiction and
brokenness. Abba we ask that, through what
You do in their lives, people everywhere would
know that You are the Lord, and that You have
brought down the things that exalted themselves
against You, and You have raised up the lowly
before You. Father thank You that You have
dried up what was green, and made the dry to
flourish. We speak life over the youth that
where they have been dead and dry in the past,
You will cause them to come to life. Abba we
ask that You would put a desire in each one of
the hearts of the youth to be the seed that falls
into the ground and dies that they might bring
forth a bountiful harvest. Father thank You that
You are the Lord and You have done it. We
decree over these precious children that they are
tender shoots in Your hand. Father thank You
that You are calling out what was dead in them
and raising the lowly on high!

(Ezekiel 17:22-24, John 12:24)

# CALLING

Thank You for the mighty men and women of valour You have created the youth to be; that You have created each one of them to tear down the idols and sexual immorality, both individually and corporately. Jesus we pray that the youth would speak the things You have commanded them, because Your commands lead to eternal life! Whatever these youth will say will be what You Abba, tell them to say - the very words of God! Holy Spirit would You guide these youth into all truth and that they would even begin searching for the deep hidden things of God! Would you teach the youth to articulate their words, so there would be fluency, so that others can understand the message that You are pouring through each one of them. We pray for ears to hear for these messengers and their hearers; let them be fully dedicated to You and the teaching of the apostles, breaking of bread, and to prayer! Come Lord Jesus COME!!!

(Judges 6:12, John 12:49-50, John 16:13, Acts 2:42, Revelation 22:20)

# IDENTITY

Thank You Jesus for the beautiful story that You
have written for each youth. Thank You that
You are with each one, that You are the Mighty
One who will save. Thank You Jesus that You
are rejoicing over them with gladness, that You
are quieting them with Your love and rejoicing
over them with singing. Abba, we ask that the
youth of this generation would be consecrated to
You, even from childhood; that they would
encounter You, hear Your voice, and
wholeheartedly run for You with childlike
innocence and childlike faith. Jesus, You
promised that the kingdom of heaven belongs to
those who are like the children! Would You so
draw even the babies and young children and let
Your hand be heavily upon them, even like it was
on Samuel. Let them hear You, Daddy. Open
their eyes to see You, and let them feast on Your
goodness! Let each one be a marked one, set
apart for You Jesus, and let them fall in love
with You even now. In Jesus' name.

(Psalm 139:16, Zephaniah 3:17, Jeremiah 1:5,
Matthew 19:14, 1 Samuel 3:3-10, Psalm 34:8)

# KNOWING JESUS

Jesus, we thank You that each child is fearfully and wonderfully made.  Thank You that You purposed and planned each life before they were even born, and every day of their lives is written in Your book.  Don't let them be hindered from coming to You, Jesus.  We ask Jesus, that their childlike faith would not be stolen from them, but that each one would and love You, and from childhood know the Scriptures, which are able to make them wise for salvation through faith in You.  God, You marked John the Baptist and filled him with the Holy Spirit before he was even born, so we ask that in the same way You would mark the youth for Your glory and Your kingdom.  Let the high praises of God be in their mouths and a double edged sword in their hands.  Thank You Jesus, that from the mouths of infants and babes You have perfected praise and established strength because of Your foes, to still the enemy and the avenger.  Abba, mark each one, so that they would never fall away, but love You from childhood; that their eyes would be fixed on You and never turn away, in Jesus' name.  Jesus, we ask that the youth would enter the kingdom of heaven like a child and that they would be humble before You, because You say that whoever humbles himself like this child is the greatest in the kingdom of heaven.

(Psalm 139:14-16,  Matthew 19:14, 2 Timothy 3:15, Luke 1:15, Psalm 149:6, Psalm 8:2, Hebrews 12:2, Matthew 18:2-4)

# INTIMACY

Daddy thank You that Your desire is toward the children. Thank You that You long for an intimate relationship with each one of them. Jesus we ask that they would all make You the most precious thing to them and call You their Beloved. Abba would You put a deep desire in their hearts to love You and know Your love. Father may they so love You that they keep Your commandments and long for Your words. Father even at a young ages, may the youth realize that You are the only One worth chasing after and pursuing, that Your Kingdom is the one worth seeking. Abba may they pursue after You like the merchant seeking the most beautiful pearl. Father would each one truly look for You knowing that You are more beautiful than any other pleasure they could desire. Father we ask that they would find You and give up everything else they have so that they might have You. Jesus we declare over the youth that they are ones like David whose one thing that he desired was to dwell in Your house and inquire in Your temple. We declare that they will be ones like Mary who will choose the one thing that really matters- to sit at Your feet, listening to You, loving on You, worshiping You. Father we ask that their gaze would be so set upon You that they would constantly make Your heart skip a beat.

(Song of Solomon 7:10, Job 23:12, Matthew 6:33, Matthew 13:45-46, Psalm 27:4, Song of Solomon 4:9, Luke 10:42)

# ONENESS

Jesus, we lift up this generation to You.  Thank
You that You will use these young ones to
increase Your kingdom to bring You honor and
glory, in Jesus' name.  Jesus, we ask that You
would be the One thing their hearts are set on;
be the One thing that they are seeking after.  We
ask that this generation would forsake all for the
sake of Christ.  Lord, keep them from loving
things of the world.  We ask that You would fill
their minds with the things of God.  Give them
visions and dreams.  Jesus, we ask for a double
portion of anointing and authority for the youth
that wherever they go, Your kingdom will come.
Darkness will be forced to flee because You and
the youth are one; where You go, darkness has
to flee, so where the youth go darkness has to
flee.  We call forth these youth to be ones who
pick up their cross and follow You.  Jesus, when
You say, "Whom shall we send and who will go
for us?" let this generation be one who will
immediately respond, "Here I am, Lord. Send
me".  Teach the youth to abide in You like You
do in the Father.  Pour out Your love on them.
Let them be entirely consumed with the radical,
life-giving love of Jesus that they couldn't do
anything but live in that love and pour it out for
Your kingdom's cause.  Thrust these mighty men
and women of God into Your harvest field.  We
declare that these will be ones like Eleazar who
will rise up quickly and strike the enemy even if
their hands are weary and cling to the sword, and
You, Lord, bring about a great victory that day

through these youth and those coming after them will only return to carry away the spoil. Thank You that they are trailblazers. Fill the children with the fear of the Lord that no matter what, they will not back down and cower, but will rise up as ones who will be faithful with everything that You entrust them with and they will be ones to whom You will say, "Well, done good and faithful servant. Enter into the joy of your Lord." Mark this generation right now, Abba. Don't let them wait. Call the youth right now. Set them free God to release Your freedom, fire and purity across the globe. Let Your burning love, fire and passion possess and consume these burning ones!

(Psalm 27:4, Matthew 16:24-26, Matthew 9:38, 2 Kings 2:9, Isaiah 61:7, Isaiah 6:8, John 17:23, John 17:26, 2 Samuel 23:9-10, Matthew 25:23)

## NATION SHAKERS

DAY 332

Jesus, we ask that the youth of our generation will quickly find that You are the only thing that will satisfy; that their hearts will long for You, and only You. Jesus we pray their desire, even as little children, will simply be to dwell in the courts of the Lord and to gaze upon Your beauty. We ask that each eye be opened to see You, Jesus. Let them behold You! Jesus let these youth be marked for Your Kingdom, for Your glory and Your honor. We ask that they will be ones who will walk in holiness all the days of their lives, that they would not turn to the right or to the left, but that their eyes will ever be fixed on Your face; that they will find the narrow road quickly. Thank You that these youth are nation shakers, that You have destined them for greatness. Father, would You place Your hedge of protection around each one, that the enemy not be able to find them, in Jesus' name. Would You keep them hidden, Abba- even like Esther- until Your time. Raise them up Papa, and let them know You and be known by You.

(Psalm 84:2, Psalm 27:4, Matthew 7:14, Esther 4:14, Exodus 33:12, John 17:3)

# FREEDOM

LORD may the praise of this generation's lips
continually go before Your throne in love &
adoration of You, the King of kings and LORD
of lords. May they continue in Your word and
become a disciple of Yours. We declare that the
men and women of this generation will know the
truth of Christ and His gospel and it will set
them free from the bondage of sin and death
that we are all born into. Abba may they receive
the revelation that all who commit sin are a
servant to sin and a servant does not remain in
the house forever, but a son does remain
forever. Therefore, Jesus we ask that You set
them free even at these tender ages, so that they
will truly be free.

(John 8:31-36)

DAY 333

# HOLINESS

Father we decree over each youth that they are ones who will hear and recognize Your voice even as children. Father we ask that they would listen to You calling their names and say like Samuel, "Speak, for Your servant is listening." Father may they be ones who give themselves to You as Your servants even as little children, and be ones that You can share Your heart with and tell things that others don't want to hear. Abba would You give each one open ears to hear You. Father may they hear Your heartbeat and be ones to whom You can entrust Your message; that they will speak forth boldly what You are telling them. Father would You give each one a clear trumpet sound to call the church back to You in holiness. You say out of the mouths of infants You have perfected praise, so may these youth be ones who will praise You in spirit, in truth, in holiness and in a way that will bring Your conviction and a deep desire for more of You to those who are living in compromise. Father may they see the plumbline of the King and walk boldly in holiness, in Jesus' name. We decree over the youth that they are ones chosen by the King. Father raise them up as young men and women who will love You from now on, that they will not fall into dissipation before finding You, but that they will come to You with the purity and simple faith of a child.

(1 Samuel 3:3-10, 1 Timothy 4:12, Matthew 21:16, John 4:23, Ephesians 1:4)

DAY 334

# INTIMACY

Father thank You for the youth. We declare over each one that they are ones who bring You great joy. Father we decree over them that they are ones who will love much, realizing that they have been forgiven much. May they be the ones who would love You so extravagantly, pouring their most precious ointment on You. We declare that the youth will walk in great faith and be saved. We decree that it has been given to each one to know the secrets of the kingdom of God, that seeing they may truly see, and hearing they may understand. We decree over them that they have the mind of Christ. Holy Spirit we ask that You would teach them and guide them into all truth, bringing to their remembrance everything Jesus has spoken to them. Would You raise up these young men and women to be ones who would not only understand the mysteries of heaven, but would be able to teach them to others. We decree that they will not remain on baby food, but that they are ones who will understand and go after the meat of God's Word, even as young children. We declare a sound mind over each one!!!

(Luke 7:37-50, Luke 8:10, 1 Corinthians 2:16, John 16:13, John 14:26, 2 Timothy 1:7, Colossians 3:2, Hebrews 5:14)

# OBEDIENCE

Jesus, thank You for the youth's amazing bursts
of joy, life and energy! Thank You for the gift of
leadership and the fun personalities that You
have given them. Jesus, thank You that before
the foundation of the world You predestined
them to be conformed to Your image. Jesus, we
ask that You would teach them to obey You in
all things. Let them be children of whom it is
known that what they do is pure and right. Jesus,
even though You are the Son of God, You
learned obedience through what You suffered
on earth, so we ask that You would teach the
children how to obey. Let them be ones who
walk in outrageous honor and humility. Let the
same mind be in each one that was also in Christ
Jesus, who did not think equality with God a
thing to be grasped, but took on the form of a
servant and was made in the likeness of men.
You humbled Yourself and became obedient to
the point of death, even death on a cross. Jesus,
thank You that these youth are ones who will
reap an abundant harvest for Your kingdom.
We call forth that promise over their lives in
Jesus' name. Let the seeds sown in their lives fall
on good soil, so that they will be ones who bear
much fruit for the glory of Your name!

(Romans 8:29, Proverbs 20:11, Hebrews 5:8,
Philippians 2:3-8, Luke 8:8, Psalm 126:5)

# LOVE

Thank You Jesus, for Your love and Your faithfulness. Jesus, let the youth be ones who never turn away from You. Let them love You with everything that they are and be ones who will never bow the knee to Baal. Jesus, even though many will fall away, let these youth be ones who always stay by Your side. Let them be ones who will not defile themselves, who will follow the Lamb wherever He goes. Let them be ones who have been redeemed from mankind as first-fruits for God and the Lamb, and in their mouths let no lie be found. Let each one be holy and blameless before You, Jesus. Thank You that You chose them before they were even born and that every day of their lives were written in Your book. Encounter the youth with Your love that will change them for the rest of their lives. Let them come to You without hindrance for to such belongs the kingdom of Heaven.

(1 Timothy 4:1, Revelation 14:4-5, Psalm 139:16, Matthew 19:14)

# FRUIT OF THE SPIRIT

We speak over the youth's lives the decrees of
God. They are ones who will walk by the Spirit
and will not carry out the desire of the flesh.
LORD we call forth the leading of the Holy
Spirit in their lives, so that they will not be under
the confines of the law. LORD open their eyes
to clearly see the difference between the flesh
and the Spirit. We pray that they will reject the
things of the flesh- sexual immorality, moral
impurity, promiscuity, idolatry, sorcery, hatred,
strife, jealousy, outbursts of anger, selfish
ambition, dissensions, factions, envy,
drunkenness, carousing, and the like. Abba
Your word is clear that those who practice such
things will not inherit the kingdom of God. Holy
Spirit come and fill the youth with the fruit of
Your Spirit which is the very thing that opposes
the flesh- love, joy, peace, patience, kindness,
goodness, faith, gentleness, and self control.
Abba against such things there is no law because
these are the very fulfillment of it! LORD You
have said that those who belong to Jesus have
crucified the flesh with its passions and desires;
may this be so in the youth, so that they will not
only live by Your Spirit, but will follow You
everywhere You lead them.

(Galatians 5:16-25)

# NEW CREATION

Father we decree over the youth that they are ones who are chosen to be raised up with Christ.  Abba we declare that they are ones who will seek those things which are above, where Christ is sitting at the right hand of God; that they will set their minds completely on things above and not on things of the earth.  We declare a death to the old youth in Jesus' name; that their lives will be hidden with Christ in God.  Jesus thank You that You are the life of the youth and that they will appear with You in glory.  We decree over this generation that all impurity and wickedness will have no hold on them in Jesus' name, but instead that they would learn to put to death anything that is earthly in them.  We decree wholeness, purity and love over their lips; that all that they speak will be true and honest and good.  We decree that the youth are ones who will completely put off the old man with their deeds and will put on the new man who is renewed in knowledge according to the image of Jesus who created them.  We declare over this these ones that they are part of Christ, where Christ is all and in all.  Father thank You that You have chosen the youth as the elect of God, holy and beloved.  Father we ask that You would draw this generation and do a miracle of holiness in their lives; that they would begin to put on tender mercies, kindness, humility, meekness and patience.  We decree that they are ones who will bear with others and be quick to forgive, just as Christ has forgiven them; that they are ones who will do just as Jesus did!  We decree that this generation is one that will walk in perfect love, which binds everything together in perfect harmony.  Father we are asking that the peace of Christ would begin to rule in their hearts, because they have been called to this!!!  Abba place a thanksgiving in the children's hearts knowing the salvation and calling that You have for them!  Father may the word of Christ dwell in them richly.  Father raise them up to teach and admonish others with all the wisdom of God, even in singing songs of praise to You with thankfulness to You!  Father we decree over this generation that everything that they do, in word or deed will be done in the name of the Lord Jesus!!!

(Colossians 3:1-17)

# IDENTITY

Jesus thank You for the youth.  Thank You that
You have called them to be holy as You are holy
and perfect as You are perfect; ones to seek You
in the hidden place, to know You and to be
known by You!  Holy Spirit thank You that You
will be the Comforter of the youth and will guide
them into all truth!  Thank You for Your will for
the lives of these youth, with plans of prospering
them and not harming them, plans of a hope and
a future!  Thank You Jesus that Your plans
consist of spending hours upon hours with
YOUR loved ones- every moment of everyday!
Jesus would You show each one of the children
that they are loved, and that You will continue to
seek after them with all Your heart and that it
totally pleases You when they will do the same!
Jesus would You rise the children up to preach
Your word with boldness and truth.  Give them
the spirit of wisdom and of revelation, so that
they may know You better!  Jesus would You
reveal to them that if they believe, they will see
the immeasurable greatness of the power that
works towards them and those who believe.
Holy Spirit reveal the Son and the power of the
cross to this generation, so that they can know
what YOU have done for them.  Jesus help them
to find JOY in the journey, knowing that the
JOY of the Lord is their strength!  Amen!

(1 Peter 1:5, Matthew 5:48, Matthew 6:6, John 16:7,
Jeremiah 29:11-14, Ephesians 6:19-20 ,
Ephesians 1:17-21, Nehemiah 8:10)

DAY 340

# OBEDIENCE

DAY 341

LORD may the song of the heart of this
generation be that You are good in every season
of their lives. LORD help them to guard their
steps when they go to the house of the LORD.
Abba help the youth to see that it is better to
draw near to You in obedience then to offer
sacrifice because that is the heart of the fool-
they unknowingly do wrong. May You be a
guard for their souls and their lips, so that they
will continually wait patiently before they do or
say anything and that they will boldly come to
Your throne with the things You have placed on
their hearts. Let them then approach Your
throne of grace with confidence, so that they may
receive mercy and find grace to help them in
their time of need.

(Ecclesiastes 3:1-8, Ecclesiastes 5:1-2)

# IDENTITY

Abba we thank You, and we praise You that
You see the children, and You know them.
Thank You Jesus, that You hear their faintest
whisper and know the deepest cries of their
hearts. Thank You Jesus, that they are the apple
of Your eye, that the youth are Your treasured
possession, and that You gave up all You had to
purchase them. The children are Your pearl of
great price! We ask, Jesus, that You give the
children a revelation of their value- how much
each one of them means to You. Father let them
base their worth on the cross! Jesus, let them see
the beauty of the cross and the intensity of Your
love that was spilled for them that day. Let them
look into Your eyes that blaze like fire, and see
the fierceness of Your love for them! Jesus You
have searched the children and known them.
You know when they sit and when they rise; You
perceive their thoughts from afar. You discern
their going out, and lying down; You are familiar
with all their ways. Before a word was on their
tongues, You knew it completely, O LORD.
You hem the youth in-behind and before; You
have laid Your hand upon them. Such
knowledge is too wonderful for them; too lofty
for them to attain. Abba, where can this
generation go from Your Spirit? Where can
they flee from Your presence? If they go up to
the heavens, You are there; if they make their
beds in the depths, You are there. If they would
rise on the wings of the dawn, if they were to
settle on the far side of the sea, even there Your

hand will guide these precious ones; Your right hand will hold them fast. If they says, "Surely the darkness will hide me and the light become night around me," even the darkness will not be dark to You; the night will shine like the day, for darkness is as light to You. You created the inmost being of every child; You knit them together in their mother's womb. Let the children praise You, Abba, because they are fearfully and wonderfully made; Your works are wonderful; let them know it full well. Thank You Jesus for the vastness of Your good thoughts toward this generation, and we ask, Abba, that the youth hear even just a few of your thoughts toward them and be enraptured forever by Your endless love for them, in Jesus' name.

(Psalm 139:1-18)

# RADICAL LOVE

Abba raise up this generation as radical lovers. Abba may the youth live completely without "balance" in their relationship with You; completely, radically, over the top in love with You, given wholly to You; hearts undivided. Father may they not fear man who dies who is but a breath, nor fear him who can only kill the body, but let this generation fear You only!!! Let them be ones so in love with You that they would even be willing to look out of their minds for You. Father may they not be afraid of the foolish things which confound the minds of the wise, but be willing to look foolish for the sake of the gospel. Draw them deep into Your river. Father may the youth not stop at going ankle deep, or knee deep, or waist deep in You, but may they give themselves to You, giving up control and letting You take them wherever You want to go! Father we decree that the youth are ones who will not be held back or stopped by the criticism of others, but will radically, purely love the King.

(Psalm 86:11. Matthew 10:28, 2 Corinthians 5:13, 1 Corinthians 1:27-29, Ezekiel 47:3-6, John 12:3-7)

# VOICE FOR THE VOICELESS

Father we ask that the youth and children of this generation be ones who will open their mouths for the speechless, in the cause of all who are appointed to die. Let them open their mouths and judge righteously and plead the cause of the poor and needy. Father we pray for a great boldness in the youth to speak for those who have no voice, even if it may not be popular. We pray Abba, that You would grant the children the ability, with all boldness, to speak Your word by stretching out their hand to heal, and that signs and wonders may be done through the name of Your holy servant, Jesus. We pray, Abba, that these ones will truly seek You with all their hearts, so that they may find You, and that out of the overflow of their relationships with You countless others will be touched and rocked because of You. Thank You, Father, that You have called this generation to so much more than status quo. Thank You that You are their light and their salvation; You are the strength of their lives, so the children don't have to be afraid. Jesus let the children be ones who will truly believe that they will see Your goodness in the land of the living; that they may not lose heart, in Jesus' name.

(Proverbs 31:8-9, Acts 4:29-30, Psalm 27:1, Psalm 27:13)

# REGENERATION

Abba, so many of the youth believe that they are saved when they are not because they attended church or said the sinner's prayer. So many believe that because they operate in signs and wonders or have received gifts from Your Holy Spirit that this is what marks and qualifies them for salvation as though this was the evidence of regeneration. Abba, Your word is clear that salvation includes a new heart and a new spirit within us. LORD, You said that many will come to you in the last days and proclaim, "LORD, LORD, didn't I…" Abba, it has nothing to do with our works or Your amazing gifts that You have given to mankind; it has everything to do with relationship and loving YOU! You said that loving you is that we would not only obey Your commands, but that it would not be a burden for us to fulfill. LORD, how many try with complaining and heavy hearts to obey You and can't because it is only possible if Your Spirit resides in the person. The flesh of man cannot do it! This is why all credit and all glory is Yours and Yours alone, because outside of You the youth would proclaim like Paul, that they are wretched and are doing the things they do not want to do, and do not do the things that they want to do! But Abba, those that are truly Yours proclaim the next few verses, "Who will set me free from the body of this death?  Thanks be to God through Jesus Christ our Lord!" Jesus You have set the youth free from sin and death.  Help them to believe it LORD!  Your word even says that You will even give life to our mortal bodies.  Therefore, there is no excuse for living lawlessly as though Your grace and sacrifice were not sufficient for the youth to truly set them free from sin and death!  LORD, let this be the generation to truly believe You and live it out!

(1 Corinthians 12:8-10, Ezekiel 36:26, Ezekiel 11:19, Matthew 7:22, 1 John 5:2-3, Ephesians 2:8-9, Romans 7:14-25, Romans 8:11, Romans 8:2)

# WIND & FIRE

Jesus, blow Your winds of fresh fire and renewal over the youth in this region. Abba, we pray that You would continue to confirm Your word to them through Your messengers this week, and that revival and awakening would burst forth for Your glory God! God, cause a shout from the youth to be released that would cause the enemy to flee from their lives. Jesus, we ask for a fresh anointing for your messengers as they love on the youth through a fresh revelation of Your love for them. In the mighty and glorious name of Jesus! Amen.

(John 3:8, Ezekiel 37:9, Hebrews 1:7, Numbers 10:35)

## PRAISE

Jesus, we know that You encompass Your
people and You surround them with Your shield
of love and favor.  LORD, we call out for a
generation that will praise You!  Holy Spirit,
would You teach the youth how to praise You to
the point that You can't help but stand in their
midst.  Abba, teach them how to sing Your
praises that will throw confusion into the
enemy's camp and cause the devil to flee!
LORD, may this be a generation that lavishes
their praises on You, so that the rocks don't have
to cry out!  You are so worthy of all honour and
glory and praise!

(2 Chronicles 20:22, Psalm 22:3, Psalm 67:3,
Luke 19:40)

# HUMILITY

Jesus, thank You for the generation that You are rising up. Let these chosen ones complete Your joy by being of the same mind as You are Jesus. Let them be of one mind together in You; having the same love and being in full accord. Let the youth be ones who do nothing from rivalry or conceit, but in humility, let them count others more significant than themselves. Let each of them look not only to their own interests, but also to the interests of others. LORD, we pray that the youth would have Your mind; the mind of Christ! You took the lowest place and fulfilled the will of the Father, even to death on the cross. Let them be ones who will do all things without grumbling or questioning You. Raise them up as blameless and innocent children of God without blemish even in the midst of a very crooked and twisted generation and let them shine as lights in the world. Abba, let them proclaim the words of Your mouth that are righteous, because there is nothing crooked or twisted in You. Let them shine Your character in purity, simplicity and truth, in Jesus' name.

(Philippians 2:1-8, Philippians 2:14-15, Proverbs 8:8)

## EXAMPLE

Jesus, we thank You that there is no condemnation for those who are in You.  Thank You that the law of the Spirit of life in You has set us free; set the youth free, from the law of sin and death.  Thank You that You did what the law could never do.  Thank You, Abba, that by sending Jesus, You condemned sin in the flesh in order that the righteous requirement of the law might be fulfilled in us who walk not according to the flesh, but according to the Spirit.  Jesus, we know that those who live according to the flesh set their minds on the things of the flesh, but we ask, Abba, let these mighty young men and women of Yours be ones who will walk according to the Spirit, setting their minds on the things of the Spirit.  Give each one the radical revelation, Jesus, that if they are in You, they have the mind of Christ!  We praise You, Jesus, that Your blood is fully enough; that You made a way for each of these youth to literally walk in Your footsteps, imitating You, and successfully following Your example.  Thank You for the call of righteousness and holiness that You have placed on them.  Jesus, we ask would You draw them now, and make them new, that each one may be a living example to the believers, calling the body back to Your holiness, in Jesus' name.

(Romans 8:1-5, 1 Corinthians 2:16, 1 Timothy 4:12)

# ENCOUNTER

Abba, we ask that You would give the youth a
desire for You; a hunger and a thirst for
righteousness that they may be satisfied. Teach
them how to ask and seek and knock, Abba, that
they may find You. Would You encounter each
one of them, Jesus. Reveal Yourself to them
that they may see that You are so much more
than a religion, more than a building, more than
a set of rules. Abba, You so loved each one of
the youth that You gave Your only begotten
Son, that whoever believes in You should not
perish but have everlasting life. You did not
come to condemn them, Jesus, but that through
You they might be saved! Open their eyes to see
the real You, Jesus, not the myriad of
misrepresentations the world has set before
them. Heal their hearts, Jesus, and set this
generation free that they may see and
acknowledge that You are alive and zealously
pursuing each one of them. Abba, let each one
of them become so enamored by Your goodness,
and the beauty of Your holiness, that any false
teachings that are preached about You would
not even begin to deceive them because they
have beheld the true King, and there is no one
like You!

(Matthew 5:6, Matthew 7:7-8, John 3:16-17,
Matthew 24:5)

# LOVE

Jesus, would you raise up a generation that truly loves. You are so clear that we love You only because You have first loved us. May the youth so experience You for themselves that they can truly love You. Thank You Jesus for manifesting Your love toward us by dying for us, so that we might live through You. We pray that the youth would so know this love, so that they can also love one another. No more wishy-washy, mamby-pamby "love" that has no action and no fruit. You said to love You is to obey You and it's not a burden. You said to love You is to be like You in the world. You said to love You is to not fear. You said to love You is to love one another. You said that it's impossible to love You and the things of the world because we will hate one and love the other. Raise up the fiery ones who will love You as You have loved us; laying down every right, every entitlement, every privilege, and becoming nothing, so that we might live. May the youth become nothing, so that their generation might live.

(1 John 4:17-19, 1 John 4:9-12, 1 John 5:3, Philippians 2:5-8)

# RIGHTEOUS JUDGMENTS

Thank You, Jesus, that all the words of Your
mouth are righteous; there is nothing twisted or
crooked in them. Let the youth understand and
know that all Your ways are straight and right to
them. Let them take instruction instead of
silver, and knowledge rather than choice gold.
Nothing that they can desire can compare with
wisdom, so let this generation, young and old,
long for Your wisdom. LORD, let them not
despise Your discipline, or be weary of Your
reproof, knowing that You reprove those whom
You love, and as a father those whom You
delight in. Let them wait for You, LORD, in the
path of Your judgments and let Your name and
remembrance be the desire of their souls. We
pray that the youth would yearn for You in the
night; that their spirits within them would
earnestly seek You, knowing that when Your
judgments are in the earth, the inhabitants of the
world learn righteousness. LORD, in Your
mercy do not show favor to those who are doing
wickedness because then they will not learn
righteousness, but discipline them that they may
come to You, see Your majesty and bear the
fruits of righteousness.

(Proverbs 8:8-11, Proverbs 3:11-12, Isaiah 26:8-9,
Hebrews 12:11)

# INTIMACY

Jesus thank You for how beautifully You created the youth . We ask Jesus, that You would be this generation's great obsession; that the one thing that the youth desire in life and the one thing that they fight for would be to dwell in Your house all the days of their lives, to behold Your beauty and to inquire in Your temple. Let them know and experience that even just one day with You is far better than a thousand days at the best vacation spot on earth. You are the only One who satisfies. Jesus don't let this generation be satisfied with anything less than all of You! Let them know for themselves that they would rather be a doorkeeper in the house of the Lord than to dwell in the tents of the wicked. Jesus we ask that these young men and women would be ones who do not walk in the counsel of the ungodly, nor stand in the way of sinners, nor sit in the seat of mockers, but let their delight be in Your law, that day and night they would meditate on it and that they would turn at Your correction. We declare, according to Your promise, that the youth will be blessed, that they will be like trees planted by streams of water, who bear their fruit in season and whose leaves do not wither and that everything they do for the glory of Your name will prosper. Jesus, we declare that these youth are ones who will fight for intimacy with You and not quit until they see You face to face. They will not settle with "good" or "better than average". This generation will fight for the gold- knowing You face to face- until they are victorious.  Thank You, Jesus, that the children are more than conquerors through You who loves them.  These are ones who will seek after wisdom even though it costs them everything they have, they will seek it diligently knowing You promise that if they seek wisdom diligently they will find it.  The youth are ones who will spread the aroma of Christ, to You first Abba, and then to others; that wherever they go everyone will clearly see that they love Jesus!

(Psalm 27:4, Psalm 84:10, Psalm 1:1-3, Philippians 3:10-14, Romans 8:37, Proverbs 4:7, Proverbs 8:17, 2 Corinthians 2:14-15, John 13:35)

# HOPE

Jesus, thank You that You are Hope and life. Right now we pray for the youth and the children to wake up and see the hope and destiny that You have for them. Thank You for the future and hope that You have purposed for them. Thank You that before they were even born, every day of their lives were recorded in Your book and You are excited about Your life for them. We pray that those whose hearts have grown sick because of their deferred hope will come alive and be filled with vision again that their dreams may be fulfilled. We know that where there is no vision the people perish, so we ask that You restore the hopes and dreams into this generation once again. Wake them up to dream the dreams of God and believe that Your destiny and purposes are possible. Fill them with hope to see beyond their present situations. We thank You that You promise that if they will call upon You and come and pray to You that You will hear them and if they seek You with all their hearts they will find You. Restore their fortunes, O GOD. Gather them from all the nations and places where You have driven them and bring them back and raise up prophets in the land.

(Jeremiah 29:11, Psalm 139:16, Proverbs 13:12, Proverbs 29:18, Jeremiah 29:12-15)

# ENCOUNTER

Jesus we pray that the youth would see You,
because we know that seeing You and
encountering You is what changes everything. It
was when Paul encountered You that he became
one of the most radical followers that ever lived.
It was when Zacchaeus saw You that he was
saved, totally changing his life around. Isaiah
saw You and was completely undone, and it was
seeing You that put the cry in his heart, "Here
am I, send me." God, when the merchant saw
the pearl of great price he was willing to sell
everything he had in order to buy it. Jesus, we
are asking for those kinds of radical encounters
for the children and the youth of our generation,
that they will see something in You that will
cause them to not care about anything else, that
they may gain You and be found in You. Put a
hunger in them like Zacchaeus had that they will
do anything to catch even a glimpse of You.
Help them to fix their gaze unwaveringly on
You. Jesus, we pray that the love that they have
seen and experienced in You would cause them
to love You enough that they can endure to the
end and be saved. May they be so focused on
You continually that life to them is Christ, and
death is gain. Thank You that these ones are
radical lovers who will die that they might live
because their eyes have seen the King.

(Acts 9:4-9, Luke 19:1-10, Isaiah 6:1-8,
Matthew 13:45-46, Philippians 3:8-9, Hebrews 12:2,
1 John 4:19, Matthew 24:12-13, Philippians 1:21,
Matthew 16:25)

DAY 255

# WORSHIPPER

Father, we ask, would You raise up a generation who will lay down their lives to love You; who will willingly pour out more than a year's wages of perfume on Your feet because they so love You. Jesus, You Yourself said that the Father is seeking those who worship Him in Spirit and in truth, so we ask, Abba, let this be a generation that so loves You that they catch the eye of the King. Let this be a generation that loves You so well that the whole house is filled with the fragrance of their worship poured out on You. We declare that their ears will be stopped to the voice of the accuser; that their focus will ever be on the face of the King who loves them and gave Himself for them. Thank You Jesus, that You are raising up the lovesick worshippers; those like Mary will set aside the works, the distractions, the busyness of ministry, and simply sit at Your feet listening to You, gleaning from You, and loving on You. Let these youth be ones who will choose the better thing which cannot be taken from them! You are so beautiful, Jesus! We ask, let these be the ones whose one thing will be to dwell in Your house all the days of their lives, to gaze upon Your beauty, and to inquire in Your temple. We praise You, Jesus! Be glorified in this generation, God!

John 12:1-8, John 4:23, Galatians 2:20, Luke 10:38-42, Psalm 27:4

# JUST DO IT

Jesus, we pray that this generation would not
wait to feel qualified, but will obey You simply
because You said "Go." Thank You that You
did what the law could never do, condemning
sin, so that Your righteous requirements of the
whole law could be fulfilled in the youth as they
do not walk according to the flesh, but according
to the Holy Spirit! Abba, we pray that they
would not set their minds on earthly things, but
on the things of God, knowing that having their
mind set on You is life and peace. Abba, we
pray that they would grab a hold of everything
for which You have grabbed a hold of them.
Jesus, You created them to be Your soldiers,
going about their Father's business every
day. Father, we pray that they would not get
caught up in the same old, same old but that they
would see the glory to which You have called
them; to bring You honour and glory, and see
Your Kingdom come on earth! Abba, You have
given such a responsibility and honour to Your
people to represent You and carry You to the
world, so we pray that the youth would see the
calling of God on their lives and be conformed to
the image of God. Jesus, You have called them
to walk just as You walked on the earth, so we
pray that this would be a generation who will
actually take You at Your word and live in the
fullness that You created them for!

(Romans 8:2-6, Philippians 3:12, 2 Timothy 2:4, Luke
2:49, Romans 8:28-29, 1 John 2:6, Ephesians 3:17-18)

# MIGHTY WARRIOR

Jesus, thank You for how amazing You created
each youth.  Thank You for the desire that You
have given them to go after You even alone in
the secret place.  Jesus, we ask that You would
teach them, like David, to worship You on the
hillside.  Take them to such a level of intimacy
with You there, where new songs of praise and
worship and adoration to You would be birthed
simply out of a place of love for You.  Through
that we ask that You would prepare the youth to
defeat the giants.  David never trained to fight a
giant, but You taught him in the secret place
how to fight the lions and bears and then when
You told him to go and fight the big one, his
trust in You was strong enough to win a victory
not only for himself, but also for his entire
nation.  Jesus, we ask that You would remind the
youth that time spent alone worshipping You is
not time wasted, but that worship is a weapon.
Let the high praises of God fill their mouths.
Jesus You called David, who took care of his
father's sheep, to slay the giant and be the king
of the land, and to father the bloodline of Jesus;
You called Gideon, who was the of the weakest
clan in Israel and the least in his Father's house
to lead an army of only 300 men to defeat an
innumerable army; and You called Paul, who
was totally against You to be one of the greatest
apostles for Jesus in history and to write a large
portion of the Bible.  Jesus we thank You that
just like these men You are calling this
generation.  Thank You for calling each one to

lead with courage, boldness, integrity, purity, and love, in Jesus' name. Thank You that You are raising up a generation of young people who will not let others look down on them because they are young, but they will set an example for the believers in speech, in life, in love, in faith and in purity, in Jesus' name. As they seek after You diligently, thank You that they will find You. Don't let them quit. Let the youth be ones who will ask You until they receive; who seek until they find; who knock until the door is opened to them. Let them so hunger after righteousness, knowing that those who hunger and thirst for righteousness will be satisfied. Let none of them be satisfied with anything less than all of You Jesus, and the intimacy and love that You have for them to walk with You. Jesus, just like David, let the youth be ones who know and believe the promises You have given them, and fight for these promises, and won't stop believing and fighting until they see them come to pass in their lives. Give the youth love to forgive anyone who hurts or hates them along the way, in Jesus' name. Thank You, that Your love is greater than that. Jesus, let these be ones who do justly, who love mercy and who walk humbly with their God. Thank You Jesus, AMEN.

(1 Samuel 16:17, Psalm 149:6, Judges 6:11-7:26, Acts 8:1-3, Acts 9:1-22, 1 Timothy 4:12, Matthew 7:7, Matthew 5:6, Matthew 5:44, Proverbs 25:22, 1 Peter 4:8, Micah 6:8)

# CALLING

Father thank You for Your mighty warriors!
Father we ask that You would establish them.
We decree that the youth are ones who will know
the power of the gospel and not be ashamed of
it. Father thank You that it is the power of God
for salvation to each one who believes You.
Father thank You that in it Your righteousness
is revealed from faith to faith, and we decree that
the youth will walk justified and righteous as
they live by faith. Jesus we ask that You would
continue to reveal the glory of the gospel to the
youth, that they would have the full revelation of
what You have purchased for them!!! Father,
thank You for their desire to pursue after You,
and we decree that they are ones who will press
on to lay hold of everything for which Christ
Jesus has laid hold of them. Father we ask that
the youth would forget those things which are
behind and reach forward to the things which are
ahead, pressing toward the goal for the prize of
the high calling of God in Christ Jesus!!! We
decree that these are ones who will so grab a
hold of You that they will be an example to all
the church of the calling that they have- to walk
in purity in life, speech, love, and in faith. We
decree that the youth are ones who will not settle
for less, but will pursue You with everything that
they are!!!

(Philippians 3:12-14, 1 Timothy 4:12, Romans 1:11,
Romans 1:16-17)

# PERSECUTION

Jesus, thank You for the youth. Thank You that Your eyes are on the righteous, and Your ears are open to their prayer. But Your face is against those who do evil. Now who is there to harm them if they are zealous for what is good? But even if they should suffer for righteousness' sake, they will be blessed. We decree that this generation will have no fear of the enemy, nor be troubled, but in their hearts they will honor Christ the Lord as holy, always being prepared to make a defense to anyone who asks them for a reason for the hope that is in them. They will do it with gentleness and respect, having a good conscience, so that if they are slandered, those who revile their good behavior in Christ may be put to shame. For it is better to suffer for doing good, if that should be God's will, than for doing evil.

(Psalm 34:15-16, 1 Peter 3:12-17)

# COMMITMENT

Father we thank You that the youth have been created to be warriors. Thank You that You promise that You are the one who trains their hands for war and their fingers to fight. Father would You raise up this generation to fight and not give up. Would You teach each youth how to fight well. Jesus You said that the Holy Spirit would come and teach us all things and bring to remembrance everything that You have said, so we're asking that even in the quiet place when they are all on their own, that Holy Spirit, You would teach them everything about who You are, and who they are, and what Your heart is. Father give each one ears to hear what You are saying to them, that even if no one else is teaching them that they would be trained at the feet of Jesus. Father may their greatest joy be to sit at Your feet and listen to You. We decree that the youth are ones who will not be deceived because they have studied You and learned Who You really are and have spent time with You in the secret place. Abba we ask that You would continue to stir up a fire and a love in their hearts that they would cry out, "Though none follow, I will follow." Thank You Jesus that they have a commitment that does not depend on anyone else, but they are choosing to follow You for themselves.

(Psalm 144:1, John 14:26, 1 John 2:27, Luke 21:8, John 6:67-69)

# ENDURANCE

Abba we seek You for this generation of youth, that since they are surrounded by so great a cloud of witnesses, that they would lay aside every weight and the sin which so easily ensnares, and let them run with endurance the race that is set before them. LORD may they look to Jesus, the Author and Finisher of faith, who for the joy that was set before Him endured the cross, despising the shame, and has sat down at the right hand of the throne of God. Jesus, let them see the prize set before them, and run for it, not looking to the right or to the left. You are the Pearl of Great price Jesus, and You are worth giving everything for.

(Hebrews 12:1-2, Matthew 13:46)

## DEVOTED

Jesus, thank You for the youth. Your eyes are searching to and fro looking for those who are of the LORD, to strengthen those whose hearts are fully committed to You. May they be fully committed to You and trust You in everything! Your eyes are on the righteous, and Your ears are open to their prayer, but Your face is against those who do evil. Help them to be righteous as You are righteous, and holy as You are holy! Thank You that this is a generation of laid down lovers who will be zealous for what is good and innocent of evil. Thank You that when this generation suffers it will be for righteousness sake and they will be prepared to give an answer for the hope that is in them!

(1 Peter 3:12-17, Romans 16:19, Proverbs 3:5-6)

# TEACHING

Abba, thank you for the youth. Thank You that You so desire to be one with them, as You are one with Jesus, closely knit together. Jesus, we thank You that You knit each one in their mother's womb, and You so desire to knit them together with You in the secret place. Abba, we thank You that You are JUST and Your decisions are right and TRUE, no matter how they feel or what trials that come their way. Teach the youth to walk according to your commands and follow after Your precepts, no matter how hard they get! Teach them how to humble themselves and seek Your face and turn from their wicked ways, so that You would hear from heaven, forgive their sin and heal their region. Let them not hold anything back from You, may they lay it all at Your feet Jesus, because of who You are and not what they can receive from You. Let the youth not be found in error of the scriptures, or lacking in knowledge of Your power. May they know the truth that will set them FREE!!! Thank You for each youth You are sending into the labour field and we declare, Your Kingdom COME, YOUR will be done here on earth as it is in heaven. AMEN.

(John 8:32, Matthew 22:29, Matthew 6:10, John 17:21, Psalm 139:15, Matthew 6:6, 2 Chronicles 7:14)

# NEXT GENERATION

Thank you so much Jesus for this coming generation of youth! The mighty men and women of God!!! Thank You that You are training them in the way they should go, so they will not depart from You when they are older. Jesus, we ask that each youth would bear much fruit and that it would remain because they abide in You. We declare each youth be made into a good tree and its fruit good. Abba, out of the abundance of the heart the mouth speaks, so make their hearts pure! We declare that this will be the generation where the distinction between the righteous ones and wicked ones begins. The good person out of his good treasure brings forth good, and the evil person out of his evil treasure brings forth evil. We ask this generation would be mindful of the words they speak, so that when they give account for their words they would be justified!

(Matthew 12:33-37, Malachi 3:18, John 15:4-5, Proverbs 22:6)

Thank you for standing in prayer with us
for this generation!

THANK YOU

# NOTES

# NOTES

# NOTES

NOTES

# NOTES

_____

_____

_____

_____

_____

_____

_____

_____

_____

_____

_____

_____

_____

_____

_____

_____

_____

_____

_____

_____

_____

_____

_____

NOTES

# NOTES

NOTES

# NOTES

_____
_____
_____
_____
_____
_____
_____
_____
_____
_____
_____
_____
_____
_____
_____
_____
_____
_____
_____
_____
_____
_____
_____

NOTES

Made in the USA
Middletown, DE
23 July 2017